• *Studies in American Biblical*

Theology as Cultura

The Achievement of Julian Hartt

• Studies in American Biblical Hermeneutics 12 •

Theology as Cultural Critique

The Achievement of Julian Hartt

by
Jonathan R. Wilson

MERCER

ISBN 0-86554-522-7   MUP/P148

□ □ □

The paper used in this publication meets
the minimum requirements of American National Standard
for Information Sciences—Permanence of Paper
for Printed Library Materials, ANSI Z39.48-1984.

□ □ □

Library of Congress Cataloging-in-Publication Data
Wilson, Jonathan R.
Theology as cultural critique :
The achievement of Julian Hartt / by Jonathan R. Wilson
xx+xxxpp. 6x9" (15x23 cm.).
(Studies in American biblical hermeneutics ; 12).
Includes bibliographical references and index.
ISBN 0-86554-522-7 (pbk.; alk. paper).

* * * Unavailable at press time. * * *
* * * Will appear in subsequent printings. * * *   CIP

Contents

Editor's Preface

This book by Jonathan Wilson fills a long-standing gap in the Studies in American Biblical Hermeneutics series. What has been lacking until now are the building blocks for the construction of a theology of culture that are themselves shaped by the nuances of the life of faith in the American setting. Julian Hartt, "the great undiscovered American theologian" who has labored as so many on these shores in the shadow of the Continent, is presented to us in this lucid and evenhanded book. The categories of thought and general orientation Hartt generated is the stuff of penetrating cultural criticism and critique. Wilson has provided us a great service in laying bare the broad outline of the thought of Hartt, the teacher and colleague of James Gustafson, Gordon Kaufman, Diogenes Allen, Ray Hart, and Stanley Hauerwas. One senses here that we are standing at the beginning of something significant in the rediscovery of so dynamic and careful a thinker, and that this book will contribute greatly to bringing Hartt into the mainstream of American theological discourse.

Let me note some basic aspects of Hartt's thought discussed in this book that seem to me peculiarly American and of primary interest to the readers of this series. Above all, Hartt's emphasis on "participatory" or practical theology strikes at the core of the American experience. He sees participation as the essence of life and takes that vision as a fundamental building block of his theology. Certainly, America perennially is the culture whose thinkers prioritize the experiential over the "merely" intellectual. As Hartt illustrates, that fact need not imply the anti-intellectualism as such that so many assume to be part and parcel of the American scene. In fact, such concepts as commandment, righteousness, indeed ethics itself, have traditionally stood at the taproot of the American theological imagination. In that sense, we have always been "rather Jewish" (as Sydney Mead once called the religion of the American republic), even in our Christian formulations. For Hartt, as with many of the greatest of American theological minds, the kingdom of God is something primarily to be done, and, in that sense, is something accessible to us. As such, Hartt stands as a major native resource for finding the unity between the intellectual and the practical, which many have traditionally espoused but far fewer have obtained on the American scene.

In large part, the praxeological emphasis in Hartt's theology is maintained by emphasizing a relentless gospel realism. He confronts us with a theology that is thoroughly and absolutely gospel centered. This implies that such contemporary commonplaces as the historical-critical analysis of the Bible, various prevailing metaphysical systems of thought, and the various ideologies of our general culture, are all placed in a subsidiary and secondary role to the gospel. The gospel is grounded in the reality of history, becoming thereby not only basis for understanding God, but for a realistic appraisal of contemporary society. The intent behind this gospel-centered theology is the formation of a prophetic church, one which diagnostically sifts through whatever various cultural particularities shape and form us, and identifies those aspects that are "lies and illusions." Hence, in the words of Wilson, "all of Hartt's work is directed toward a single aim: to witness to the Kingdom of God and thereby to expose the illusions of a world in order to save the present age."

This discussion of the practical leads necessarily to the question of theology and the church. Here Wilson shows how Hartt maintains a separation between these two distinctive aspects of the faith. While a vigorous theology is crucial to enable the church to carry out its mission of proclaiming the gospel, it is not dependent upon it for its vitality. Ultimately, both theology and church serve the kingdom, and both embody it only imperfectly. Thus, the twin dimensions of faith—the formation of Christian community and theological reflection—while standing in mutual solidarity, do so independently. This is a perspective sorely needed in the contemporary expression of Christian life. It is a time when the church comes under intense criticism as, for example, "America's most segregated hour," or the bastion of a kind of warmed-over political correctness. Even more serious is the brute fact that the church is largely ignored by the American intelligentsia. Wilson shows us that a number of Hartt's reflections have the potential to lead us back to a meaningful public theological discourse, one that does not retreat from the world but engages it fully from the standpoint of the gospel. For Hartt, no cultural expression ought to displace the centrality of the Christ event, the Lord of both human particularity (history) and the providence of God (cosmos). It is a solid rock upon which to build an American theology of culture that is both meaningful and long-lasting.

Ecumenical Theological Seminary, Detroit   *Charles Mabee*

Preface

In this book, I seek to retrieve the work of Julian Hartt and argue that from him we must learn that theology that is faithful to the Gospel of Jesus Christ is "theology as cultural critique." Hartt's practice of theology as cultural critique is grounded in his convictions about the Gospel but the concept of theology as cultural critique arises from Hartt's analysis of "theology of culture." In this analysis, Hartt, by attending to the claims of the Gospel, transforms concern for culture and for theology of culture into a theological critique of culture that serves the church's commission "to preach the gospel of the kingdom in Christ."[1]

At one time in the twentieth century, debates about "theology of culture" brought together an otherwise diverse group of theologians. Among these theologians were Paul Tillich, Richard Kroner, H. Richard Niebuhr, Reinhold Niebuhr, Nicholai Berdyaev, Emil Brunner, Bernard Meland, and Julian Hartt. In the midst of their diverse accounts of culture and its place in the work of theology, these theologians all wrestled with the particularities of the culture in which they did theology. This recognition of the "cultural situatedness" of theology is a crucial development.[2] Prior to this time, although theology was always done in particular settings, its situatedness had not been a problem. Now, however, the situation is recognized as a problem for theology: how can theology, which purports to be about the eternal, unchanging Gospel, be done in particular situations? To what extent does a particular situation shape theology? What about particular theologians—how does a situation shape them? From another direction, what responsibility does theology have for responding differently to changing situa-

---

[1]*TTE*, 9.
[2]I will develop the notion of "situatedness" in chap. 1.

tions? All of these questions may be gathered up by asking, what is the status of "culture" in theology?

Theology of culture comprises the varied answers to these questions. Although the phrase "theology of culture" has faded in use, the problems that it identified are still with us in David Tracy's public theology and in George Lindbeck's cultural-linguistic proposal. It is also reflected in the many diverse theologies among us today. Where the early discussion tended toward a monolithic, hegemonic definition of culture, today's theologies have broken that hegemony in favor of a more careful delineation of the many situations. Feminist, Womanist, African-American, Hispanic/Latino, and other theologies are part of the trajectory of theology of culture. Still one more point on the trajectory may be identified in those theological works that are concerned with "everyday life."

Each of these theologies continues the concern with the place of "culture" in theology. Where before we had debate about "theology of culture," today we have "theologies of cultures." I am not at all interested in restoring the hegemony of the previous discussion; nevertheless, the question of cultures remains with us and presents the most challenging questions for theology. Moreover, questions about cultures have come to hold a predominant place in other intellectual work, in the rise of cultural studies, critical social theory, sociology of culture, and other similar practices. In this situation, I will argue, the work of Julian Hartt has much to teach us for the continuing work of theology.

Julian Hartt received degrees from South Dakota Wesleyan University, Garret-Evangelical Seminary, and Yale University. After completing the Ph.D. at Yale University in 1940, with a dissertation on "The Ontological Argument for the Existence of God," he taught at Berea College for three years. He then returned to Yale, where he taught for the next twenty-nine years. During that time he became Noah Porter Professor of Philosophical Theology and chaired the University's Department of Religion. In 1972 he moved to the University of Virginia as Kenan Professor of Religious Studies, from which position he retired in 1982. During his years at Yale and Virginia, Hartt published numerous books, articles, and review essays (see the bibliography), and influenced a number of contemporary theologians who were his students and colleagues, among them James Gustafson, Gordon Kaufman, Stephen Crites, Diogenes Allen, Ray Hart, David Bailey Harned, Stanley Hauerwas, and Dennis Campbell. He was respected (and even feared) for his erudition and rhetorical skills. The questions that concern us in this study are the questions that pervade his work. Indeed, I did not bring an interest in theology of culture and an understanding of theology as cultural critique to Hartt's work; rather, they arise from my study of his work.

In chapter 1, I introduce Hartt's theology and relate it to theology of culture, arguing that Hartt conceives and practices theology as cultural critique. This argument is developed and supported in the following chapters as I seek to lay bare the fabric of Hartt's theology.

In chapter 2, I show how the Gospel serves as revelation, foundation, and authority in Hartt's theology and display the unique features of Hartt's treatment of these issues. Here I am concerned not so much with placing Hartt in his historical context as with indicating the continuing relevance of his work. In particular, I argue that Hartt's notion of the Gospel as the revelation of God *and the human situation* is an elegant move that enables a powerful account of the Gospel as the foundation and authority for theological critique of culture.

In chapter 3, I examine Hartt's re-presentation of the Gospel of the Kingdom in the preaching, person, and work of Jesus Christ and show how this Christological essay is also an illuminating exercise in cultural critique. These two chapters belong together as an argument for Hartt's understanding of the Gospel and of theology as cultural critique. At the end of chapter 3, I accentuate three aspects of the Kingdom which are revealed in the Gospel and which are of particular importance for Hartt, namely, the actuality, intelligibility, and dialectic of the Kingdom. Together, these three aspects of the Kingdom direct Hartt's practice of theology as cultural critique.

In chapter 4, I show how these three aspects of the Kingdom shape Hartt's account of the church in relation to the Kingdom, to culture, and, more specifically, to "Christian" civilization and American culture.

In chapter 5, I do the same for his account of the world by attending to Hartt's description of how we construct cultures and civilizations and how the actuality, intelligibility, and dialectic of the Kingdom demand and enable a theological critique of cultures.

My purpose in chapters 2–5 is to commend Hartt's theology by displaying his analytic powers and the coherence of his work, so that others may appropriate his work for today. Throughout these chapters, Hartt's erudition and comprehensiveness tempt one to comment continually on the relevance of his thought for problems and proposals in contemporary theology. I have resisted that temptation because the relevance seems obvious and commentary on it pedantic and distracting. I trust the reader to make those judgments for herself or himself.

In chapter 6, I bring together the various strands of my argument in order to describe the achievement of Julian Hartt. I go beyond a mere summary of Hartt's theology in order to identify four characteristics of his work that produce its insight and power and serve as models for a contemporary theological critique of culture: evangelizing the imagination, transforming history, replacing metaphysics, and asserting the truth of Christian believing. On each of these issues I compare him to various other accounts presently on the theological scene in order to show the strengths of Hartt's theology. I then conclude the chapter with a summary critique of Hartt's theology of culture.

In many conversations with other theologians about Hartt's work, I have encountered great enthusiasm for his theology. One of those theologians, Ralph Wood (who knows Hartt's work well and is a mature theologian of culture himself), described Hartt in a private conversation with me as "the great undiscovered American theologian." In this work, I hope to display some of Hartt's greatness and promote a more sustained and public discovery of his theology than has previously prevailed.

• Acknowledgments •

This work began as a dissertation at Duke University. Thomas A. Langford, who supervised the dissertation, was a gracious guide and made many suggestions for its improvement. Stanley Hauerwas suggested the topic to me and gave a lot of time and effort in helping me through my many struggles with Hartt's thought. The other members of my dissertation committee, Dennis Campbell, D. Moody Smith, Jr., and Thomas Spragens, contributed to this work through their courses and through private conversations with me. Dennis Campbell, dean of the Divinity School, generously shared his time and his enthusiasm for Hartt's theology with me. Moody Smith's seminar on the quests for the historical Jesus contributed greatly to my understanding of Hartt's Christology. Thomas Spragens's courses in political theory gave me an appreciation for our culture and introduced me to debates about the "situated self."

Prior to Duke, the faculty and students of Regent College, Vancouver, encouraged me to enlarge my world and my ambition. I am indebted to professors Bruce Waltke, Carl Armerding, Ward Gasque, Larry Hurtado, Ian Rennie, James Houston, and Roy Bell, and to students such as Craig Broyles, Steve Pattee, and Brian Campbell.

During and since my time at Duke a circle of friends has been crucial to my life and thought: Greg and Susan Jones, David Cunningham and Teresa Hittner-Cunningham, Andrew and Margaret Adam, Phil and Kim Kenneson, Reinhard Hütter and Nancy Heitzenrater Hütter, and Stephen and Melinda Fowl.

Andrew Adam suggested that I contact Charles Mabee about publishing my work in Studies in American Biblical Hermeneutics. Charles's enthusiasm, encouragement, and guidance have contributed greatly to this work. American theology owes him a debt for conceiving and editing the series. We are also indebted to the editors at Mercer University Press for sustaining the series and keeping the volumes in the series affordable.

After completing my work at Duke I have been encouraged to continue my work on Hartt by many scholars, most notably by James Gustafson, Ralph Wood, Diogenes Allen, and Douglas Ottati. They, however, may disagree profoundly with my interpretation of Hartt's theology.

Finally, my wife Marti Crosby and our daughter Leah willingly and joyfully made my graduate education a part of their lives for three years. Since then, they have tolerated, supported, and encouraged me during a difficult transition to college teaching. Since my wife, a Canadian, continually and enthusiastically offers a critique of "American culture," she is partly responsible for the topic of this book. She bears no responsibility, however, for the fact that, in spite of her best efforts, I cannot escape being American; such is my particular situation. I can only rejoice in what Julian Hartt has taught me: no cultural situation is beyond the redemptive work of God's Kingdom.

Abbreviations
of Works by Julian Hartt

CC   *A Christian Critique of American Culture: An Essay in Practical Theology*. New York: Harper & Row, 1967.

LIM   *The Lost Image of Man*. Baton Rouge: Louisiana State University Press, 1963.

RQ   *The Restless Quest*. Philadelphia: United Church Press, 1975.

TCU   *Theology and the Church in the University*. Philadelphia: Westminster Press, 1969.

TMI   *Theological Method and Imagination*. New York: Seabury Press, 1977.

TTE   *Toward a Theology of Evangelism*. New York: Abingdon Press, 1955.

*Dedicated
to
Marti Crosby Wilson*

Chapter 1

Situating Hartt

> God demands that His church stand out against the world and yet be prepared to sacrifice itself for real human beings in the real world. The church is under a divine obligation to so preach the Gospel of Christ's Kingdom that the native love of illusion and fear of truth will be understood in their intimate interrelatedness. This interrelatedness is part of the fabric of everyday. This does not mean that the church should despise the everyday as inane or demonic. Rather, everyday is to be offered up to the redemption of Jesus Christ. This offering-up occurs in the faithful praying of the church. That is the beginning and the end; but there is much for the church to do in the middle.[1]

Some of the most enduring and influential works of theology have been written, wittingly or unwittingly, in response to particular cultural circumstances. Augustine's *City of God* (written in response to the fall of Rome), Thomas's *Summa* (shaped by the Middle Ages and the rediscovery of Aristotle), and Calvin's *Institutes* (driven by the Protestant reformation and the need to expose several heresies) were shaped by their culture, yet they exercise considerable influence on contemporary theology.

In more recent times—since the rise of forces reflected in Schleiermacher's *Speeches* (1799)—this recognition of the influence of particular circumstances has led to the rise of "culture" itself as a problematic for theology. That is, theology has turned its atten-

---

[1]Julian N. Hartt, *A Christian Critique of American Culture: An Essay in Practical Theology* (New York: Harper & Row, 1967) 48.

tion to the very nature of "culture" and its significance for the work of theology.

One way to expose what has been going on in theology is to borrow a notion from recent political philosophy. In his critique of Rawls's *Theory of Justice*, Michael Sandel introduces the notion of the "situated self."[2] In contrast to Rawls's ideal self, which is shorn of all particularity behind a "veil of ignorance," the "situated self" is the person who has an identity shaped by his or her history, social standing, education, economic advantages or disadvantages, etc. All humans, Sandel argues, are situated selves. Therefore, one cannot, as Rawls proposes, shear off the particularities of a person in order to achieve a "veil" of some sort of neutrality or a universal self.

Although this specific language has not been used, the situated self and, in particular, the situated theologian has occupied theology for the last two centuries. Indeed, the situation may be more acute for the theologian than for the political philosopher: Christianity claims that the Gospel is eternal truth, so how are we to relate this eternal truth and changing cultures? Not only the theologian, but the Gospel itself is situated. Of course, this problem has many ramifications, but before we consider them, we should note that recognition of this dilemma extends back beyond the past two centuries.

In Psalm 137, Israel's theologians wrestled with their situation:

> By the waters of Babylon,
> there we sat down and wept,
>   when we remembered Zion.
> On the willows there
>   we hung up our lyres.
> For there our captors
>   required of us songs,
> and our tormentors, mirth, saying,
>   "Sing us one of the songs of Zion!"

---

[2]Michael J. Sandel, *Liberalism and the Limits of Justice* (Cambridge: Cambridge University Press, 1982).

> How shall we sing the Lord's song
>   in a foreign land?   —Psalm 137:1-4 RSV

What is Israel to do with the song of Zion now that she finds herself in Babylon? What is she to do with a theology shaped by the promised land when she finds herself in another land, in a new situation? Can she, should she, continue to sing the old song? Should she sing in the language of Babylon? Should she drop the old song and learn the song of Babylon?

Theology has confronted similar questions in recent years. Although this entire work is dedicated to exploring these issues, we may note them here in a preliminary way. First, theology has recognized that the church is always situated in a particular culture and given a particular responsibility for that culture—it is to proclaim the good news of Jesus Christ to all places and times. Secondly, theology has recognized that the Gospel itself is "situated." Jesus Christ, the center of the good news, was an Israelite male living in Roman Palestine. Moreover, the church which gave us the record of the Gospel in the New Testament was shaped by its places and times. Given this double-barreled recognition of the situation of the church and of the Gospel, the task of theology becomes immeasurably complex.

This complexity has given rise to much of the church's theology. In the past two hundred years the situatedness of Gospel and church has been a particularly acute theological problem, construed in many different ways.[3] One of the earliest construals, Lessing's famous dictum that "accidental truths of history can never become the proof of necessary truths of reason,"[4] sets reason over against history, i. e., over against the situatedness of Gospel and church, and seeks to shed all aspects of the faith which partake of

---

[3]I recognize that "situatedness" is a rather inelegant term. The more common alternative, "situation," connotes more the notion that this or that situation is a problem. Here I use situatedness to indicate the problematic nature of the recognition that the gospel and the church are always, everywhere, situated.

[4]Gotthold Lessing, "On the Proof of the Spirit and of Power," *Lessing's Theological Writings*, ed. and trans. Henry Chadwick (Stanford CA: Stanford University Press, 1972) 53.

situatedness, of contingency.[5] Following Lessing, many theologians sought to identify those aspects of Christianity which conformed to and expressed the necessary truths of reason.[6] Other theologians gave different construals of and answers to the problem of situatedness.[7] For example, toward the end of the nineteenth century Ernst Troeltsch wrestled with this problem and bequeathed it to twentieth century theology as the problem of history.[8]

In the course of these debates, the problem has become a complex of problems. What is the role of historical criticism in theology? What is the relationship between historical knowledge and metaphysical knowledge? What is the relationship between Gospel, church, and culture? How does one justify Christian belief? What is the nature of faith? All of these questions, and more, have animated theology for many years and have been shaped by our recognition of the situatedness of theology.

In North America, two theologians, Paul Tillich and H. Richard Niebuhr, have been particularly sensitive to the cultural situation of Christianity and have been dominant forces in the shaping of theology. Even today much of the theological work being done in North America may be traced to the influence of one of these two giants. The present work, however, is devoted to exploring, as an alternative to Tillich and Niebuhr, the theological work of one of their younger contemporaries, Julian Hartt.

---

[5]For an informative analysis of Lessing's thought, see Gordon E. Michalson, Jr., *Lessing's "Ugly Ditch: A Study of Theology and History* (University Park: Pennsylvania State University Press, 1985).

[6]A full catalogue of these responses is given in Colin Brown, *Jesus in European Protestant Thought 1778–1860* (Durham NC: Labyrinth Press, 1987).

[7]It is not my purpose here to track all of these responses. All of nineteenth- and twentieth-century theology can be read as responses to or denials of the situatedness of Christianity.

[8]See the various writings of Troeltsch, in particular the essays collected in *Ernst Troeltsch: Writings on Theology and Religion*, ed. Robert Morgan and Michael Pye (Atlanta: John Knox Press, 1977). An influential description of Troeltsch's impact on twentieth-century theology is Van A. Harvey, *The Historian and the Believer: The Morality of Historical Knowledge and Christian Belief* (New York: Macmillan, 1966; repr.: Philadelphia: Westminster Press, 1981).

Hartt is important for our purposes because his passion and work has been animated by a recognition of the situation of Gospel and church in American culture. Hartt's response to the situatedness of Gospel and church is rooted in a concern for the church's witness to the Gospel in the world.[9] In one of his earliest works, *Toward a Theology of Evangelism*, Hartt's concern is that

> wherever the church is authentically Christian the conviction yet lives that its sole reason for existence is to preach the Gospel of the Kingdom of God in Christ. The commission is there held to be still in force, the commission to "evangelize the world." But great are the difficulties in holding this conviction purely and firmly, and the difficulties multiply daily.[10]

And in one of his latest essays, "Fallout from Shifting Winds in Doctrine," Hartt probes "for the indefeasible unity of the concrete and the universal in the utterance of the Gospel, in the articulation of Christian history-in-faith."[11] In this work we will probe Hartt's theology in order to discover how it responds to the situatedness of theology and to the demands placed upon the church by the evangelical commission (Matthew 28:18-20).

• Hartt's Theology of Culture •

Hartt's passion for the situation of theology and the church's faithfulness to the evangelical commission finds expression in his understanding of theology of culture. "Theology of culture" can mean many things and be used in many ways.[12] For some theolo-

---

[9]See Hartt's use of the Babylon imagery of Ps 137 in Julian N. Hartt, *Theological Method and Imagination* (New York: Seabury Press, 1977) viii.

[10]Julian Hartt, *Toward a Theology of Evangelism* (New York: Abingdon Press, 1955) 9.

[11]Julian N. Hartt, Sr., "Fallout from Shifting Winds in Doctrine" (photocopy, 1988) 38.

[12]In *CC* Hartt does not identify particular representatives of "theology of culture" whom he has in mind. In the conclusion to this chapter we will compare his own theology of culture to his analysis of several theologies of culture in an article, "Theology of Culture," *Review of Metaphysics* 6 (March 1953): 501-10.

gians, "theology of culture" signifies theological interpretation of "high culture," of artistic endeavors. For others, "theology of culture" signifies the theological work which identifies the elements of a society or civilization that are truly creative. In Julian Hartt's work, "theology of culture" comprises the whole of theology and commits theology to a critique of culture:

> We shall find at the heart of [our] enterprise a conviction that Christian theology is improperly done when it comes only at the end—or in homiletical forays into the arts along the way—to consider the cultural situation of faith. Theology of culture seeks to relocate and reestablish the very foundations and form of Christian theology. It is not enough for culture to appear somewhere in theological systems as a topic of high importance. Theology proper must begin with the analysis of culture, or it will prove to be systematically meaningless. The analysis, thus, is no longer conceived as a bid to attract the attention of the audience before doing the serious work. It *is* the serious theological work. Thereafter the fate both of dogma and of metaphysics—if the theologian of culture will admit any such distinction—is not hard to predict.[13]

In this description Hartt signals his awareness of the situatedness of Christian faith, the church, and theology: from beginning to end theology must be concerned with the cultural situation of Christianity.

This concern marks Hartt's work and contributes to its complexity. It means that Hartt never develops his theology in the abstract; Christology, ecclesiology, pneumatology are always developed in an intricate conversation with and critique of culture.[14]

---

[13]CC, xviii. As will be clear by the end of this book, Hartt seeks an interpenetration of culture, dogma, and metaphysics, which does not admit any clear distinctions between them.

[14]For example, in CC Hartt's Christology is developed in relation to "ontological fundamentals" of the human situation, his ecclesiology is developed in relation to American culture as a Christian civilization, and his pneumatology

But, although Hartt recognizes, in his theology of culture, the situatedness of the Christian faith, he also seeks to reorient theology of culture in accordance with the logic of Gospel:

> theology of culture is interpretation of a system of values, creations, and attitudes in the light of and on the basis of the revelation of being and good in Jesus Christ. The aim of such interpretation is very much more than to discover how far and in what ways a culture falls short of "Christian standards." The aim is to enable the church to discharge more adequately their responsibilities in the present moment. To "save the present age"; this is the aim.[15]

For Hartt, theology of culture is not simply theological interaction with "the arts" or an attempt to win a hearing from the elite "cultured despisers" of the Gospel. Nor is it a retreat to confessionalist methodology or theological relativism. Rather, in Hartt's understanding, theology of culture is the fulfillment of the evangelical commission. That is, the church's commission to be witnesses of Jesus Christ requires theology of culture. As we will see, this understanding offers an approach to the situatedness of the Christian faith which sets many issues in new light.

Although Hartt's understanding of the Gospel will occupy us in the next two chapters, we may anticipate that discussion and identify the Gospel, in Hartt's understanding, as the everlasting actuality of the Kingdom of God established and revealed in the preaching, person, and work of Jesus Christ. However, we must also note that Hartt resists essentializing the Gospel and never

---

is developed in relation to the question of revolution.

[15]Julian N. Hartt, *The Restless Quest* (Philadelphia: United Church Press, 1975) 49. Cf. *CC*, 48: "The aim of theological criticism [of culture] is not to prove that the church is right and the world is wrong. To show forth the truth in which man may rightly divine who he is and to whom he belongs and aginst whom he sins and whither he is bound; and with whom there is fulness of life from everlasting to everlasting: the elucidation of this gospel is the theological calling. . . . If this is really the aim of theology of culture we can have no serious objection to it."

gives a definition of the Gospel. Rather, in his work the "meaning" of the Gospel is unfolded in relation to various themes.

Hartt adopts his approach to theology fully cognizant of the depth of uncertainty which marks contemporary culture. The questions and doubts go beyond the problems of singing the old song in a foreign land. Now doubt is more radical: "Why did any thoughtful person ever suppose truth and wisdom could be reliably and predictably attained in those old ways?"[16] In responding to this doubt Hartt writes "from and out of a conviction that the 'faith once and for all delivered to our fathers' is true and can be construed as true. Yes, and defended as true."[17] This conviction, coupled with Hartt's concern for the cultural situation of the faith, promises a theology which brings together often disparate concerns. Indeed, one of the hallmarks and strengths of Hartt's theology is his commitment to overcoming the dualisms and disjunctions which mark theology. It is often easier to accept these dualisms and disjunctions than to attempt to overcome them. But Hartt refuses the easy way out; instead he seeks to think together, to reconcile, such issues as particularity and universality, history and metaphysics, faith and reason, kerygmatic and apologetic theology.

Earlier in this century, a number of otherwise diverse theologies coalesced around the notion of "theology of culture." Something of the character of Hartt's theology of culture can be outlined in a brief comparison with these other theological projects that may be called "theology of culture."

In Hartt's earliest application of the term "theology of culture," he distinguishes "five distinct types of theological interpretation of culture."[18] The first three types of theology of culture presuppose and proceed from a metaphysical or ontological scheme established independently of theology. Representatives of these types include: (1) Jacques Maritain and Robert Flewelling, who represent Thomism and Personalism; (2) Nicolai Berdyaev, whose ontological

---

[16]*TMI*, viii.

[17]Ibid., xiv.

[18]Julian Hartt, "Theology of Culture," *Review of Metaphysics* 6 (March 1953): 501.

program is "projected poetically and existentially, not analytically and scientifically"; and (3) Paul Tillich, who "proceeds from an established and assured phenomenological scheme" and from "ontology after the mode of Heidegger: analysis of the structures begins with the question about the 'metaphysical animal' himself."[19]

The fourth and fifth types which Hartt identifies do not presuppose a metaphysical system. Indeed, they often see metaphysics as a threat to theology. Representatives of the fourth type include: (a) Richard Kroner, who argues that only religious faith can transcend "the duality of self and world" which is the motivation for culture as an attempt at self-salvation; (b) Emil Brunner, who believes that Christianity, as the spiritual basis of western civilization, provides the answers to our culture's problems; and (c) Reinhold Niebuhr, who finds in Christianity a "conceptual scheme" which provides a "culture-transcending perspective . . . for criticism of our situation, and our idolatrous efforts to understand it (science and philosophy) and to redeem it from futility and death." The fifth type of theology of culture, represented by H. Richard Niebuhr, "proceeds from a faith that on its own confession is at once culturally conditioned and culture-transcending."[20]

Hartt differs from the first three types in his rejection of metaphysics as the *foundation* of theology of culture, though as we will see he still allows a place for (a re-placement of) metaphysics in the work of theology.[21] Hartt also differs from the variations on the fourth type. In contrast to Kroner, Hartt sees religious faith not as human mastery of culture but as human submission to God who fulfills creaturely existence. In contrast to Brunner, Hartt locates cultural transcendence not in the presuppositions of a civilization but in the Gospel; in comparison to Hartt, Brunner's

---

[19]Ibid., 501-504.

[20]Ibid., 504-507.

[21]See the discussion on the errors of theology of culture in chap. 2 on the Gospel as foundation and the explication of his "re-placement" of metaphysics in chap. 6.

position is too provincial, because it limits Christian criticism of civilization to those civilizations based on Christian presupposi-tions.[22] In contrast to Reinhold Niebuhr, Hartt does not derive a "conceptual scheme" from the Bible as the transcendent basis for theology of culture. In a subtle difference, Hartt argues that the Kingdom of God in its present actuality, not the conceptual scheme of the Bible, transcends culture. Scripture teaches us to see the Kingdom, but that work is not tied to one conceptual scheme; theology conceptualizes, but only in service to that vision of the Kingdom. In response to H. Richard Niebuhr, Hartt agrees with him that "it is not really the 'faith' that transcends culture: the faith is in God, whose purpose embraces culture, as well as nature," but argues against Niebuhr that "surely the delineation of *this* being, God, would call for some kind of metaphysical analysis and construction somewhere along the line."[23] As we will see, this difference means that Hartt rejects Niebuhr's "confessionalism" in favor of asserting and defending the truth of the Gospel.

None of these comparisons argues Hartt's position; each serves, rather, provisionally to place him on the landscape of theology of culture and to anticipate the issues which arise in his theology. For example, our anticipation of Hartt's founding his theology in the Gospel, not in metaphysics, together with his criticism of H. R. Niebuhr's lack of metaphysical analysis, promise an account of metaphysics which displaces it from its role as foundation and authority for theology but does not dispense with it altogether. Similarly, every issue that Hartt addresses in this analysis of theology of culture receives detailed and nuanced attention in his later work.[24]

---

[22]Hartt's criticisms of Collingwood are apropos. See "Metaphysics, History, and Civilization: Collingwood's Account of Their Interrelationships," *Journal of Religion* 33 (July 1953): 198-211, and "The Philosopher, the Prophet, and the Church (Some Reflections on Their Roles as Critics of Culture)," *Journal of Religion* 35 (July 1955): 147-59.

[23]Ibid.

[24]Hartt addresses the issues raised by Kroner's work in *CC*, chaps. 2, 7, and 10. He addresses the issues raised by Brunner in *CC*, 64-69, and in his analysis of Collingwood's notion of "absolute presuppositions" in "Metaphysics, History, and

However, my presentation of Hartt's theology will not begin with these issues. The problem of the situatedness of Christianity and the issues of theology of culture provide the background, not the structure, for an examination of Hartt's theology. To adopt a problem-centered approach would obscure the strength and integrity of Hartt's theology. The great strength of Hartt's work is his constructive theology which is, at the same time, cultural critique. Moreover, the bulk of Hartt's work is not, for want of a better label, "methodological," that is, Hartt did not set out to solve problems of how to do theology, he simply did it. Even his methodological essays, he warns, are not innocent of "systematic concerns." Indeed, for Hartt the most important methodological issue—"how to order the principles of the faith in such coherence, clarity, and pungency that the errors of the mind of the age can be seen in their true light and repented of"—is already formed by Christian convictions.[25]

But even this distinction between constructive theology and methodological concerns obscures Hartt's strength, because the very way in which he works undercuts that distinction. As he elucidates the Gospel, he also illuminates the methodological problems of theology, exposes their roots, weighs the options, and shifts the emphases, to mix a few metaphors—the complexity of Hartt's theology seems to require the mixing of metaphors. His theology daunts any interpreter's attempt to convey its originality and power, challenges comprehension and defies simplification.

Nevertheless, because of its originality and power, Hartt's work has much to teach us. In this book I seek to expose the central elements of Hartt's theology, to show its continuing relevance, and to encourage further discussion of his contributions by delineating three central elements of Hartt's theology of culture: Gospel, church, and world.[26] It would be easy to think of Gospel as that

---

Civilization: Collingwood's Account of Their Interrelationships," 198-211. Hartt addresses Reinhold Niebuhr's position in *TMI*, chap. 3.

[25]*TMI*, xvi, xiv.

[26]Although they pursue slightly different questions and arrive at different answers, two recent theologians also work with something similar to this triad. In

which the church uses to interpret world; however, Hartt's thought is not so tidy. He recognizes that each of these elements is being interpreted at all times. So although the following chapters will ostensibly concern, in turn, Gospel, church, and world, the other elements will always be implicitly involved in the discussion.

• Conclusion •

How shall we do theology by the waters of Babylon? In these few paragraphs I have laid out the elements of Hartt's answer that will concern us. First, fundamental to Hartt's theology are the claims of the Gospel. The Gospel is fundamental in the sense that Hartt holds his theology accountable, not to philosophical convictions, social analysis, methodological commitments, or social programs, but rather to the Gospel itself. Secondly, God commissions the church to preach the Gospel and, through the Holy Spirit, enables the church's mission. Finally, the arena of the church's mission and, in a sense which we will later explore, the objective of the Gospel, is the world. All of these elements can be gathered under the rubric of theology of culture as formulated by Hartt.

There are three aspects of Hartt's work which may frustrate our quest. First, his work is incomplete. He introduces *A Christian Critique of American Culture* as "the initial part of a theological program" but he has not produced further volumes in that program.[27] His *Theological Method and Imagination* may be read as methodological reflections on, or rationale for, the earlier work, but

---

Constructing Local Theologies (Maryknoll NY: Orbis, 1985) 20-21, Robert J. Schreiter uses this same triad to introduce a methodological proposal. What Schreiter proposes, Hartt has done. In *Text, Church and World: Biblical Interpretation in Theological Perspective* (Grand Rapids: Eerdmans, 1994), Francis Watson uses a similar triad to argue that "biblical interpretation must . . . abandon the myth of the self-enclosed text and correlate the text with the reality to which it bears witness, understanding the text as located primarily in the church which itself is located in the world" (293). Hartt's theology is entirely consonant with this argument, but adds to it an account of the Gospel as the reality to which the text bears witness, and locates the text, the church, and the world within that larger reality.

[27]CC, xi.

it also points toward "the work of systematic theology . . . [which] outranks by a great deal any and all methodological concerns and bemusements."[28] Since we do not have Hartt's "systematic theology," our understanding of his work must remain open and suggestive.

Second, Hartt "argues" by elucidation—his style is indirect and allusive. For example, Hartt does not provide us with a definition of "culture" or with formal arguments in support of his use of the concept. Rather, he simply sets his conception of culture to work, expecting its exemplification to possess coherence, pungency, and elucidatory power. This approach contributes to the interpenetration of form and substance, meaning and method, in Hartt's work. To subject it to the kind of analysis and argument practiced here may obscure that interpenetration and distort his work. We must be on guard against such distortion. But the reader is warned: this work is no substitute for reading Hartt.

Third, Hartt seldom directly identifies those with whom he is arguing. Most of his works lack footnotes (and indices), and what footnotes there are seldom identify his interlocutors. Therefore, when I juxtapose Hartt with other theologians for the sake of contrast and clarification, I am seldom trying to claim that *this* is the particular theologian whom Hartt has in mind. Rather, I will simply be utilizing this or that theologian for the clarification of a position or argument. So, for example, although Hartt never mentions H. Richard Niebuhr when he criticizes confessionalism, I will take Niebuhr as representative of that position.

Some of Hartt's reviewers speak of his work as unfortunately neglected.[29] I agree. The neglect is due in part to the taste for the

---

[28]*TMI*, xiv. Nevertheless, Hartt goes on to claim that "methodology is part of systematics" (xv). The picture is muddied further by his preference for dogmatics over systematics. See below, chap. 2.

[29]Speaking of *TMI*, David Kelsey says "Julian Hartt sketches elements of a theological position that is both fertile and genuinely distinctive, that is, not identifiable as a variant on any of the major options on the current scene." Later in the review Kelsey decribes the central section of *CC* as "a powerfully written, imaginatively original, and largely ignored Christological essay." See David Kelsey, "Christian Sense Making: Hartt's *Theological Method and Imagination*," *Journal of*

novel and *avant garde* at the time when Hartt did much of his work. It is also due in part to the difficulties I just noted. And even though Hartt's students have been immensely influential in contemporary theology, Hartt's own work has seldom been an explicit part of that discussion.

In this book, I am concerned more with rectifying this neglect of Hartt than with identifying its causes. Hartt has thought deeply and creatively about doing theology today. He has not only thought and written about how to develop a theology of culture, he has actually done it. In doing so he has remained faithful to the Gospel while living by the waters of Babylon and has transformed "theology of culture" into "theology as cultural critique."

Religion 58 (1978): 428-35. George W. Stroup also refers to CC in his review of *TMI*: "It is unfortunate that *A Christian Critique of American Culture*, which [Hartt] published ten years ago and at that time described as "the initial part of a theological program that I conceive to be Dogmatic," did not receive the critical attention and careful assessment that it deserved." See George W. Stroup, review of *Theological Method and Imagination*, in *Theology Today* 34 (1977–1978): 336-38. Finally, note James Gustafson's claim that Hartt "has one of the most brilliant and profound theological minds and spirits in the Christian community today; unfortunately, he is one of the least appreciated theologians now writing." See James M. Gustafson, *Can Ethics Be Christian?* (Chicago: University of Chicago Press, 1975) 183n.15.

Chapter 2

The Role of the Gospel in Hartt's Theology of Culture

So in the Christian faith the revelation of God in Jesus Christ stands forth as the disclosure of the shape, the form, of the real world. This form is given as something already there, that is, as fully actual. It is also an obligation binding upon my powers of enactment. It is something seen and something to be done. This is why the Christian must be prepared to argue about the shape of the real world. For him religion is a "reality game" as well as an ethical command, and it is neither to the exclusion of the other. But in his arguments with other theological options he cannot surrender his primordial acknowledgment of Jesus Christ as the being in whom the real shape of the world is disclosed.[1]

In the previous chapter we took some initial sightings of Hartt's theology under the rubric "theology of culture." I argued that although Hartt recognizes in his theology of culture the situatedness of Gospel, church, and world, he also reorients theology of culture by the logic of the Gospel. That is, Hartt's practice of theology of culture signals what Hartt understands the Gospel to require of theology: theology of culture is precisely that theology which is authorized and demanded by the Gospel; theology of culture is theology whose aims are consonant with the Gospel; and the possibility of theology of culture rests upon the Gospel.

---

[1]Julian N. Hartt, *Theology and the Church in the University* (Philadelphia: Westminster Press, 1969) 134.

Therefore, the task immediately before us is to explore the Gospel as it (1) reveals the reality to which a theological critique of culture bears witness, (2) founds a theological critique of culture, and (3) authorizes such a critique.

In the first section I examine Hartt's understanding of the Gospel as *revelation*. His construal of the Gospel as revealing, at the same time, God and the human situation, requires Christian theology to be theology of culture, that is, theology which is concerned with the human situation. Since the Gospel reveals God and the human situation, the Gospel also serves as the foundation and authority for Christian theology of culture.

In the second section of this chapter I will explore the Gospel as the *foundation* of theology by examining two notions that Hartt brings to the forefront of the theological enterprise: practical theology and the criterion of preachability. Hartt's exposition of these two notions displaces other contenders for the role as foundation for criticism of culture, such as philosophy, art, and social science. At the conclusion of this section I argue that Hartt's construal of revelation supports his development of a position that is neither foundationalist nor antifoundationalist.

In the third section I investigate the Gospel as *authority* in Hartt's work. Here we will consider how Hartt overcomes the dilemma of heteronomy versus autonomy and external versus internal authority, again on the basis of his construal of revelation.

Each of these sections is proleptic of Hartt's elucidation of the Gospel that we will examine in the next chapter. Due to Hartt's understanding of the Gospel there is no set, universal criteria by which he may commend the Gospel or his theology. The appeal of Hartt's theology is inductive and particular, not deductive and general.[2] Since the appeal is inductive, we must exercise a certain patience and restraint as the whole of the position is developed.[3]

---

[2]These assertions anticipate our later discussion of authority, below.

[3]For induction and "holism" see Jeffrey Stout, *The Flight from Authority* (Notre Dame IN: University of Notre Dame Press, 1981). In a similar vein see the notion of a cumulative argument in Basil Mitchell, *The Justification of Religious Belief* (New York: Seabury Press, 1973). In this approach, an argument does not seek to

Since the appeal is particular, each reader must discover for herself reasons to reject or accept Hartt's claims.[4]

• Gospel as Revelation[5] •

Although the concept of revelation has come under heavy fire in modern theology, Hartt does not abandon it.[6] Instead he calmly analyzes the position of revelation and the lines of support for it, showing that the situation is not as grim as often reported. Hartt's construes the concept of revelation in such a way that many of the dilemmas that plague modern theology may be approached in new ways and perhaps even overcome, by arguing that "in the Christian faith the revelation of God in Jesus Christ stands forth as the disclosure of the shape, the form, of the real world."[7]

---

establish an indubitable or even probable premise which then guarantees the truth of a position which is logically inferred from that premise; nor does an argument work piecemeal. Rather, the justification of a position depends upon the whole argument, and upon many different kinds of "evidence." For Hartt, the kind of argument that can be made for Christian believing derives from Christian convictions. In other words, the shape of the case for Christian believing depends upon Christian convictions. Thus, Hartt roughly resembles Stout's induction and holism, but he is not a thoroughgoing antifoundationalist. He is closer to Mitchell's cumulative case.

[4]For the notion of authority as particular, see Nicholas Lash, *Voices of Authority* (Shepherdstown: Patmos Press, 1976) 42: "The absolute always speaks to us in the accents of the particular, and our reluctance to accept the implications of this is perhaps an expression not so much of obedience to truth as of sloth or personal insecurity. To confess the authority of Christ is, or should be, to confess one's willingness to live, and think, and work in a world in which there are no 'easy answers.' It is to live by hope."

[5]A fuller version of the following discussion appeared in Jonathan R. Wilson, "The Gospel as Revelation in Julian N. Hartt," *Journal of Religion* 72 (October 1992): 549-59.

[6]See the survey of the vicissitudes of the doctrine of revelation in Ronald F. Thiemann, *Revelation and Theology* (Notre Dame IN: University of Notre Dame Press, 1985) chaps. 1–3. I discuss Thiemann below.

[7]*TCU*, 134.

Hartt's use of the doctrine of revelation ties together his concern for the evangelical commission of the church and theology of culture:

> The church bears witness to God's revelation. It preaches God the Revealer. And it preaches that God the Revealer and God the Transcendent are one God.[8]

> The revelation of God in Jesus Christ is the absolute authority upon which the Christian must stand as a critic of the contemporary world.[9]

But there is a subtlety in Hartt's use of the doctrine of revelation that is difficult to identify and describe.

For example, in a review of Hartt's *Theological Method and Imagination*, David Kelsey claims that

> Hartt stands closer to those for whom theology is an explication of what it is to be a believer (possessor of "God-consciousness"; of "faith's self-understanding"; of "ultimate concern") than to those for whom it is an explication of something objective to which the believer responds ("revelation"; "Word of God"). The subject matter of theology is emphatically not revelation (p. 77).[10]

But Kelsey's claim, though not clearly erroneous, obscures the originality and power of Hartt's conception of revelation.

In an early essay on "The Situation of the Believer" Hartt summarizes his analysis of revelation:

> What, then, is known in Revelation? A situation, not simply one Being who somehow produces that situation. God is the infinite and eternal in that situation; I am an integral self in that situation (and as such a genuine *other* to God), a self who is coming into existence through "hearing the word."[11]

---

[8]*TTE*, 20.

[9]*CC*, 62.

[10]David Kelsey, "Christian Sense Making: Hartt's *Theological Method and Imagination*," *Journal of Religion* 58 (1978): 429.

[11]Julian Hartt, "The Situation of the Believer," in *Faith and Ethics: The Theology*

Among the several convictions and commitments impacted in this statement is Hartt's overcoming of the opposition between objective and subjective which Kelsey imposes on him.[12] Because he misses this intention to overcome subject-object distinctions in revelation, Kelsey misidentifies the affinities of Hartt's theology.[13]

Earlier in the same chapter to which Kelsey refers, Hartt seeks to overcome this same subjective-objective distinction in his analysis of faith. Faith, he suggests, has three connotations:

(1) Faith denotes the content of belief. . . .

---

of H. Richard Niebuhr, ed. Paul Ramsey (New York: Harper & Brothers, 1957) 235. One is immediately reminded of Calvin's opening assertion that "nearly all the wisdom we possess, that is to say true and sound wisdom, consists of two parts: the knowledge of God and of ourselves." See Jean Calvin, *Institutes of the Christian Religion* in two volumes, ed. John T. McNeill, trans. Ford Lewis Battles (Philadelphia: Westminster Press, 1960) 1:35. However, Calvin goes on to wrestle with which part of knowledge to begin with, and concludes that "however the knowledge of God and of ourselves may be mutually connected, the order of right teaching requires that we discuss the former first, then proceed afterward to treat the latter" (ibid., 39). Calvin erred in not following his instinct to hold the two parts of knowledge together. Most theology has continued the same error and can be divided into those who choose one starting point and those who choose the other. This approach achieves a certain clarity at the expense of obscuring the reconciliation of God and humanity disclosed by the Gospel.

[12]In this Hartt draws on the work of Austin Farrer. For a helpful discussion of this relationship see William M. Wilson, "A Different Method; A Different Case: The Theological Program of Julian Hartt and Austin Farrer," *The Thomist* 53/4 (October 1989): 599-633. However, I think that Wilson misleads when he suggests that Farrer's case for theism, his "rational theology," is an example of Hartt's methodology in action. In my judgment, Hartt's methodology leads to a case for Christian believing, which both Hartt and Farrer agree is something far different from theism. See Austin Farrer, *Finite and Infinite: A Philosophical Essay*, 2nd ed. (Westminster: Dacre Press, 1958; repr.: New York: Seabury Press, 1979) 299-300.

[13]Kelsey further misleads because he does not sufficiently reflect Hartt's distinction between vision and worldview, Hartt's stringent analysis of the dangers of "worldview," and his preference for "vision." See *TMI*, 74-81, and below, "Gospel as Foundation." (I take Hartt's term "outlook" [*TMI*, 77] to be synonymous with vision, not with worldview.)

   (2) Faith is, or is something emerging from, a life- and world-
       transforming experience. . . .
   (3) The essence of faith is obedience. Better still, it is obedience
       joined to trust.[14]

In his analysis of these three "forms" of faith, Hartt argues that
each has something of the other in it. In the disclosure of God in
the Gospel, there is content and experience (or encounter). But
when the believer "stakes a claim" by asserting that the real shape
of the world is also disclosed and declares an intention so to
construe the world and so to act, then the three forms of faith are
bound together.

The richness of this account of the Gospel as revelation is evident throughout Hartt's work, but it is summarized in his claim
that

> in the Christian faith the revelation of God in Jesus Christ stands
> forth as the disclosure of the shape, the form, of the real world.
> This form is given as something already there, that is, as fully
> actual. It is also an obligation binding upon my powers of
> enactment. It is something seen and something to be done.[15]

In this formulation, Hartt incorporates faith as content, as encounter, and as obedience. He moves faith beyond being "merely a
function of moral commitments or an effect of psychic-social ten-
sions" to a faith which is also knowledge—of God and of the
world—which demands transformation. The claims of faith are not
our imposition of God upon the world, nor our projection of God
into our experience, nor our declaration to suppose God. Thus construed, faith and revelation are not mere expressions of the subjective, of the state or disposition of the believer. Therefore, dogma
is not merely the relevant, consistent, congruent elucidation of
"what it is to be a believer."[16]

---

    [14]Ibid., 47, 48, 51. See also *CC*, 153-59, where Hartt argues that faith comprises
"believing, trusting, and knowing."
    [15]*TCU*, 134.
    [16]Kelsey, "Christian Sense Making," 429.

However, Hartt's conception of revelation should not be construed as a return to objectivity or to "biblicist Protestantism."[17] Hartt does allow the claim that the Christian vision is sponsored by God, that in revelation God designates "how he is to be actually perceived," but he does not allow revelation to become a claim to epistemological privilege. The case for Christianity is not made by shouting "Revelation"; nor is it made by recourse to the prevenience of God as the foundation of revelation. We must "distinguish confessing that God is the cause of my outlook from making an appeal to divine warrant for the vindication of my convictions and commitments in the eyes of other human beings."[18]

Kelsey, then, is right to distance Hartt from those who conceive revelation as exclusively or primarily objective revelation of God, but he is wrong to swing Hartt to the side of those who view theology as the explication of the subjective state of the believer. Theology, for Hartt, is concerned with the situation of the believer, but that situation is *revealed* in the Gospel. Therefore, a faithful presentation of Hartt's concept of revelation must join together the subjective and objective. Indeed, while Hartt must work with these categories given by the tradition, the thrust of his work is toward overcoming them.

By mining another vein in the riches of Hartt's account of revelation, we may discover that a case can be made for Christian believing.[19] The possibility of making a case for Christian believing rests on Hartt's assertion that revelation discloses "the shape, the form, of the real world" and, consequently, that "the Christian must be prepared to argue about the shape of the real world."[20] Because the Christian believes (1) that in the Gospel God reveals Godself as Creator and Redeemer, and (2) that God commissions

---

[17]For Hartt's account of the shortcomings of biblicist Protestantism, see *TMI*, 131-32.

[18]*TMI*, 132, 160, 77. Here Hartt establishes the distinction between foundation and authority that we will explore in the next two sections.

[19]We will further explore Hartt's understanding of making a case for Christian believing in chap. 6.

[20]*TCU*, 134.

and enables the church to proclaim that Gospel, the Christian is committed to asserting the truth of that Gospel. But when the truth of the Gospel is doubted, questioned, or attacked, the Christian responds, not by simply retelling the story of Israel and Jesus, nor by adducing historical evidence for the events—the mighty acts of God—narrated in Scripture, but by showing that the Gospel elucidates the real shape of the world. Thus, in case making, revelation is not so much something to look at as it is something to see with, to look along.[21] But in this case making the Christian must not slip into some universal account of human experience or current rational consensus. The Christian's argument is still governed by the "primordial acknowledgment of Jesus Christ as the being in whom the real shape of the world is disclosed."[22] By holding together the Gospel as the revelation of God and of the shape of the real world, Hartt establishes a way to retain the concept of revelation and give reasons for the faith without falling into the inconsistencies which mark other contemporary positions.

We may sharpen this picture of Hartt's account of revelation by comparing it to the recent work of Ronald Thiemann, *Revelation and Theology*. Thiemann begins by undermining several current approaches to a doctrine of revelation. He first shows the conceptual confusions which mark three very different attempts to provide "foundationalist" justification for Christian belief in the doctrine of revelation.[23] Next, while admitting the coherence of Gordon Kaufman's rejection of revelation, he argues that Kaufman's position should not be accepted by default, that is, simply because foundationalist accounts are incoherent, especially if Thiemann's nonfoundationalist account of revelation is persua-

---

[21]See a similar account of revelation in Austin Farrer, *The Glass of Vision* (Westminster: Dacre Press, 1948). On a more popular level see C. S. Lewis, "Meditation in a Toolshed," in *God in the Dock: Essays on Theology and Ethics*, ed. Walter Hooper (Grand Rapids: Eerdmans, 1974) 212-15.

[22]*TCU*, 134.

[23]Thiemann, *Revelation and Theology*, 16-46, analyzes the work of Locke, Schleiermacher, and Torrance.

sive.[24] Then Thiemann considers the functionalist accounts of revelation developed by Kelsey and Wood and argues that ultimately their view rests upon theologians' *decisions* to construe scripture *as if* it were revelation. Such a position is impotent to provide reasons for so viewing scripture. Again, Thiemann counsels caution in adopting this position, until other options are explored.

Thiemann's own nonfoundational theology argues that "revelation is the continuing reality of God's active presence among his people."[25] In this presence God is intrinsically related to the community. Therefore, revelation is no longer the claim to God's epistemological or temporal priority which render foundationalist accounts incoherent. Revelation now has to do with the identity of God rendered by the biblical narrative. According to Thiemann, this view of revelation and Christian claims about God's identity can be justified, without returning to foundationalism, by meeting three criteria: intelligibility, Christian aptness, and warranted assertability.[26] He then seeks provide such a justification by presenting the Gospel as "narrated promise."[27]

Hartt, I think, would agree with much of Thiemann's argument. Both reject foundationalist accounts of revelation. Like Hartt, Thiemann argues that foundationalist accounts, such as those of Locke, Schleiermacher, and Torrance, confuse "*rational justification* and *causal explanation*."[28] Both Hartt and Thiemann retain the notion of revelation against Kaufman's jettisoning of the claim.[29] Although Hartt's (and to some extent Thiemann's) account is close to the functionalist account of revelation in Kelsey, I think Hartt would finally agree with Thiemann that the functionalist account

---

[24]Ibid., 49-56.

[25]Ibid., 80.

[26]Ibid., 92-96.

[27]Ibid., chaps. 5, 6, and 7.

[28]Thiemann, *Revelation and Theology*, 43; his emphasis. Cf. *TMI*, 77.

[29]Ibid., 49-56. Hartt's relationship to Kaufman is more complex than I have noted here. We will compare their projects in chap. 6.

eventually rests on the theologian's decision and thus is unsatisfactory as an alternative to the problems of foundational accounts.[30]

But Hartt diverges from Thiemann in at least three illuminating ways. Basic to these divergences is the second part of Hartt's assertion about revelation, that in revelation God discloses "the shape of the real world." Thus, while agreeing with Thiemann's assertion that Christian case making "is neither a theoretical demonstration of the universal religiousness of the human species nor a causal explanation of the origin of theological knowledge,"[31] Hartt's construal also allows him to move beyond the confession of the Christian community, beyond the coherence and congruence of the Gospel story, beyond the simple retelling of the story, to an argument over the shape of the real world.[32]

Thiemann does acknowledge that "the [biblical narrative] purports to describe the real world which we all inhabit" but he sees that as simply another assertion of God's identifiability.[33] For him, "anthropological considerations follow from the primary focus on

---

[30]Ibid., 56-70. Thiemann also considers the work of Charles M. Wood, *The Formation of Christian Understanding: An Essay in Theological Hermeneutics* (Philadelphia: Westminster Press, 1981), as a functionalist account of revelation. Although Wood differs from Kelsey at important points, for our purposes here the positions can be taken as one.

[31]Thiemann, *Revelation and Theology*, 93.

[32]There is some truth in Michael Goldberg's accusation that narrative theology like Thiemann's may be "at bottom only a sophisticated fundamentalism and thus a sophistic fideism to boot." See Michael Goldberg, "God, Action, and Narrative: *Which* Narrative? *Which* Action? *Which* God?," *Journal of Religion* 68 (January 1988): 39-56, esp. 46n.37. However, Thiemann's position has resources for answering Goldberg's accusation: "But since the narrative purports to describe the real world which we all inhabit, God's characteristic behavior must be sufficiently exemplified in this world in order for that hope to be justifiably sustained." (Thiemann, *Revelation and Theology*, 154) The weakness of Thiemann's work is that he is content to make this assertion without carrying through the project or suggesting how it can be done. The virtue of Hartt's position is that he sees that the Gospel is story, but also more than story; and he carries his project through to arguments about the real shape of the world.

[33]Thiemann, *Revelation and Theology*, 154.

God's identity and reality."[34] In contrast, Hartt holds together the Gospel as the revelation of God and of the real world, that is, of the human situation.

Therefore, Hartt also diverges from Thiemann by moving the argument about revelation away from Scripture as the sole focus. For Hartt, the argument over revelation does not alone concern the status of Scripture as revealed; it also concerns the status of Scripture as revealing. It is not enough to provide a coherent and intelligible account of how Scripture renders God's identity. Nor is it quite right first to show how Scripture renders God's identity and then seek to show how that identity renders the shape of the real world. God's identity and the shape of the real world are rendered simultaneously in Scripture. The task which devolves upon theology is the same: to render simultaneously God's identity and reality and the shape of the real world. That work is the aim of Hartt's theology of culture and sets his work in contrast to Thiemann's.

In the next two sections of this chapter we will see how Hartt's account of the Gospel as revelation also shapes his understanding of the Gospel as the foundation of theology of culture and calls for a particular account of the Gospel as authority. These two topics will continue to show the contrast between Hartt and Thiemann, as well as other theologians, and to anticipate Hartt's interpretation of the Gospel.

• Gospel as Foundation •

In their pursuit of theology, cognizant of its situatedness, theologians have sought a foundation for theology that stands outside any particular situation. Some have sought a foundation in universal truths of reason, others in universal human experience, others in the presuppositions of a particular culture, still others in a par-

---

[34]Ibid., p. 84. Thiemann's failure to consider the possibility that the Gospel renders God and the human situation simultaneously also, I think, accounts for his inability, which he confesses at this point, to place the work of Stanley Hauerwas.

ticular metaphysical scheme—the possibilities are nearly endless. Others, perceiving that the quest for a foundation is futile, have turned "antifoundationalist." As with foundationalism, the ramifications of "antifoundationalism" are nearly endless.

For Hartt, theology has a foundation, but not one that will satisfy the traditional quest for a foundation. For Hartt, the foundation of theology, and of a theological critique of culture, is the Gospel. This Gospel reveals the human situation but cannot be reduced to that situation. After explicating Hartt's understanding of the Gospel as the foundation of theology of culture, we will see how his conception offers an alternative to both foundationalism and antifoundationalism.[35]

In *A Christian Critique of American Culture*, Hartt claims that "Christian criticism is founded on the presence of God transcendent in the actual world. . . . The norm of Christian judgment of the world is then God transcendent revealed as wholly present in Jesus Christ."[36] This assertion of the Gospel as foundation of theology of culture is interdependent with Hartt's account of the Gospel as revelation of God and the human situation: persuasive criticism of culture founded in the Gospel supports Hartt's claims about revelation, and Hartt's claims about revelation make it possible to find the basis for criticism of culture in the Gospel. In asserting the Gospel as the foundation of theology, Hartt effectively denies that role to other claimants, many of which have held sway in other theological programs.[37] But he does not altogether

---

[35]For a helpful analysis of varieties of foundationalism and nonfoundationalism in theology, see Douglas F. Ottati, "Between Foundationalism and Nonfoundationalism," *Affirmation* 4/2 (Fall 1991): 27-47. I am indebted to Paul Lewis for bringing this essay to my attention.

[36]CC, 74. Hartt does not always use "foundation" and "authority" as discretely as I am in this chapter. The terms are often interchangeable in his work. My separation of the two terms is meant to identify two different aspects of his thought: (1) what is the ground of Christian theology and (2) how the authority of that ground works.

[37]In *Toward a Theology of Evangelism* (24) Hartt says:

faith in God the Father Almighty is the foundation of Christian life and thought, and it is therefore the first principle of the church's evangelical

deny insights from philosophy, art, and science. For example, Hartt uses each of those disciplines to analyze the anxiety of our age.[38]

Hartt's understanding of the Gospel as foundation and his displacement of other foundations can be explicated by examining his notions of practical theology and of preachability. This explication anticipates Hartt's interpretation of the Gospel and shows that Hartt's position is neither foundationalist nor antifoundationalist.

Practical Theology. The notion of "practical theology" has recently been given considerable attention. Hartt anticipates the rise of practical theology and in his own work ties it to his understanding of theology of culture and to his conception of the Gospel as revelation. Since the Gospel reveals God and the human situation, the task of the church is the preaching of that Gospel. The first responsibility of theology of culture is to serve that task of the church. Such theology, responsible to this practice of the church, is best described as practical theology.

---

mission. It is the foundation, but it is not the whole faith; and by itself could not account for the evangelical mission. These foundational convictions are indispensable to the essential life and work of the church, and without them the church cuts and trims its message to conform to the "philosophy and empty deceit" of the world (Col. 2:8). Nevertheless, these primary convictions are too general and sketchy to hold the whole story and to disclose the really binding part of the story. Indeed, the gospel as story does not appear at all in them. What so far appears is a kind of metaphysical background of the story and for the story. The background must be there. But if the church had only the metaphysical background, it would have no truly divine mission in and for the world.

I have quoted this at length because it may appear that Hartt first held the opinion that theology, or "Christian life and thought," was to be founded on "God the Father Almighty," and only later came to found theology upon the Gospel. However, in Hartt's theology, God is known as "the Father Almighty" through the Gospel. Moreover, Hartt is here using foundation in a different sense and in fact in the latter part of the quote he asserts that apart from the Gospel there would be no Christian mission.

[38]Ibid., 25-40. Many other examples in Hartt's work could be referenced. We will return to this issue in chap. 5.

Hartt acknowledges that "practical theology" ordinarily denoted (at the time of his writing) courses in "church management, sermon preparation, parish visitation, and, perhaps, the organization of the church school."[39] But Hartt seeks to overthrow the received notion of practical theology and the characteristic distinction between the "practical" and the "scientific" or "theoretical" theological disciplines:

> How is it possible for a religiously serious interpretation of divine revelation to be essentially theoretical and scientific? Surely the theologian organizes the propositional expressions of Christian belief with a view to exhibiting their truth. He is not trying to test a theory as a scientist does. He is not interested decisively in the purely logical connections of one proposition with another. If he builds a complex metaphysical system, as in fact some Christian theologians have, he does it neither to satisfy an aesthetic appetite nor finally to see what he can learn and recommend about God, man, and the world. If he builds a system he must do it to show forth some of the remoter implications of the revelation of God in Jesus Christ.[40]

This passage reflects Hartt's conception of the Gospel as revelation of God and the human situation and his conviction that the church's responsibility is to preach that Gospel. He rejects the priority of any theology which, through theory, metaphysics, or science, moves away from the practice of the church. Therefore, he claims that "the first fundamental venture of theology ought to be identified as practical theology because it is immediately and decisively engaged with those doctrines, those propositionally formulated beliefs, that are indispensable to the actual preaching of the Gospel of Jesus Christ."[41]

In these claims Hartt intends a reformulation of the intellectual work of theology. That reformulation does not simply involve the addition of an intellectually respectable discipline called "practical

---

[39]*CC*, 124.
[40]Ibid., 125.
[41]Ibid., 126.

theology" somewhere in the theological encyclopedia or the requirement that a theologian spell out the *"praxeological"* implications of her systematic or theoretical work. The reformulation which Hartt seeks would replace the traditional concerns of "fundamental" or "foundational" theology with the concerns of "practical theology."

Therefore, theology must first engage, and be engaged by, the Gospel. Theology's responsibilities are set by the Gospel and the practices of the church impacted in the Gospel. Because of Hartt's understanding of the Gospel, some of the concerns of traditional fundamental theology survive, though they are transformed by being derived from the Gospel rather than from some cultural situation. Thus, for example, the question of how to make the Gospel intelligible is very much a part of Hartt's theology, but the question as derived from the Gospel does not ask which philosophical system may best carry the Gospel, nor does it ask how the Gospel might be trimmed to fit "the mind of the age." Rather, the question asks the church to perceive the human situation as revealed in the Gospel and to represent that to the world.

In Hartt's discussion of practical theology he rejects "systematic theology" as the first fundamental venture in theology for two reasons.[42] First, a system is a formal achievement which, like a syllogism, may be valid but untrue.[43] Second, systematic theology incorporates material as well as formal elements worked out in response to various forms of rationality rather than in response to the Gospel.[44] Thus, systematic theology turns away from the Christian vision of the world revealed in the Gospel, to gaze upon

---

[42]As will become clear in what follows, Hartt does not reject being "systematic" in one's approach to theology. Rather what he is rejecting is the construction of a system in place of the Gospel.

[43]Ibid., 75.

[44]In *CC*, 138-43, Hartt identifies three critical mistakes made by systematic theology in assuming: "1. The subject of action is matter. . . . 2. The subject is entirely in a causal nexus. . . . 3. The meaning of time is exhausted by 'periodicity' and 'linearity.' "

the system and its propositions. As Hartt puts it with characteristic pungency:

> all the reasons for crediting the proposition "God exists" cannot prepare one for the shock of His actuality. The Gospel administers this shocking actuality. Woe to theology if it provide metaphysical insulation against it![45]

In his elevation of practical theology Hartt issues severe strictures against systematic theology, even to the point of rejecting a particular form of it.

Against systematic theology, Hartt asserts the propriety of dogmatic theology as "a conceptualization of the Christian outlook."[46] Dogmatic theology shares some concerns with systematic theology. Each is "a propositional expansion of a metaphor (or of a vision)." Each has "a stake in being and truth." Each is concerned with competing outlooks present in the culture.[47]

But dogmatics differs from systematics at crucial points. Its concern with competing outlooks is practical, since it seeks to serve Christians who must live in the world of competing outlooks. Therefore, dogmatics seeks "to clarify conviction and commitment when they need it; when that is, the behavior of the church and Christian suggests confusion, ignorance, ambiguity, failure of courage, or perversity." In this task, the dogmatic theologian stands within the Christian community and upon the fundamental conviction that the Gospel of Jesus Christ is the revelation of the actuality of God and the human situation. On this basis the dogmatician may borrow language "from commonsense discourse and from technical vocabularies" if it can be "worked loose from any of the decisions and commitments for which it was originally designed." He will also make metaphysical claims, but from a "foundation" and with a logic which "is unlikely to satisfy rationalistic appetites."[48]

---

[45]Ibid., 144.
[46]*TMI*, 77. Hartt also identifies CC as dogmatic theology (xi).
[47]*TMI*, 81.
[48]Ibid., 81, 82. Here is an indication and confirmation of the claim made in the

Hartt's description of theology as, first of all, practical theology, and his consequent rejection of systematic theology and affirmation of dogmatic theology, display his conviction that the Gospel is the foundation of theology. The first task of theology, according to Hartt, is to serve the mission of the church imposed upon it by the Gospel, not to serve some political agenda or social program or to develop some metaphysical scheme. However, to put the contrast so baldly may be misleading. Since the Gospel reveals God and the human situation, a theology that is responsible to that Gospel necessarily involves itself in politics, social agenda, and metaphysical convictions. Hartt's subtle point is that such involvement is given to theology and shaped by the Gospel as foundation.

Preachability. Hartt's description of practical theology elevates the criterion of "preachability" to preeminence. Therefore, an examination of Hartt's understanding of "preachability" will further elucidate the Gospel as foundation for a theology of culture. In some church circles a typical response to a doctrinal or ethical assertion is, "That sounds good: but will it preach?" Hartt's criterion of preachability has something of this in it, but it is also far richer.

For Hartt, "preachability is the norm of doctrinal adequacy."[49] This claim is not an appeal to the state of preaching in the church, nor is it the enthronement of relevance. Rather, "preachability" is the recognition that "the Gospel is given to the church to be proclaimed just as it (the Gospel) is. 'Just as it is' means that since the Gospel says one thing about God, the church has no authority to say anything else in its preaching."[50] Thus the criterion of preachability recognizes the Gospel as the foundation of the church and of theology. Recognizing its foundation in the Gospel, the church must continually examine whether its life faithfully represents the Gospel of the Kingdom; not just verbal proclamation

---

previous chapter that although Hartt displaces metaphysics as the foundation of theology, he does not reject it altogether. Rather, as we see in chapter 6, he puts metaphysics in service to the Gospel.

[49]CC, 131.

[50]Ibid., 132.

but the whole life of the church—including its theology—is to be judged by the Gospel.[51]

But "preachability" does not underwrite the church's withdrawal from culture or the contemporary idiom. As we will see in the next chapter, Hartt's understanding of the Kingdom as an everlasting actuality means that the Gospel is not just about a once upon a time, but also about a here and now. Therefore, in its preaching the faithful church must disclose to its hearers their situation as revealed in the Gospel of Jesus Christ.

> Moreover, since Pentecost the church has known that God the Spirit communicates to the faithful a power of communication. This is a language rather than a tongue. It is a rhetoric perfectly proportioned to the truth which it is given to express. "Every man understood what was being said." God help us but there are days when we are tempted to believe that this was the last time this has happened in any church anywhere.[52]

Thus, the criterion of preachability requires the church to be faithful to the Gospel and intelligible to the world. However, "intelligibility" is a requirement first imposed, not by the culture or some form of rationality or mode of discourse present in the culture, but by the Gospel, which reveals God and the human situation. Since the Gospel reveals God and the human situation, it contains within itself the demand for and the criterion of intelligibility.

When this drive for intelligibility is severed from such an understanding of the Gospel, the church begins to seek another foundation for its proclamation. Often, the church rightly remembers that the Gospel is about the human situation, but it forgets that the Gospel reveals that situation. Then the church begins casting about outside the Gospel for an account of the human situation in order to proclaim the Gospel intelligibly. One spurious foundation which Hartt rejects is metaphysics. Another which must be rejected is any account of "universal human experience."

---

[51]Ibid., 344.
[52]Ibid., 327.

At first glance Hartt's construal of revelation may seem to legitimize such an approach. However, two differences must be noted. First, the dependence runs in the other direction—any account of human experience given by the church is founded in the Gospel. Thus any account of human experience given by the church is particular, not universal. Secondly, what the Gospel discloses is not common human experience, but the human situation before God as revealed in Jesus Christ.[53] This human situation is "universal" in that the Gospel claims the entire cosmos as God's creation, but it is inseparable from the particularity of the revelation of God in Jesus Christ and the particularity of the times and places in which the church proclaims it.[54]

Conclusion. In Hartt's elevation of practical theology and preachability, he rejects the search for a foundation for theology outside the claims of the Gospel. In this Hartt is against foundationalism. But there are many ways of being "antifoundationalist" and Hartt's antifoundationalism, rooted in the conviction that in the Gospel God discloses Godself and the shape of the real world, is neither historicist nor relativist, though it is historical—that is, rooted in the continuing history of Jesus Christ, and relative—that is, related to the particular convictions of the church.

Hartt asserts the Gospel as the foundation of Christian criticism of culture against these options in responding to what he calls "a kink in the mind of the present age, a condition we have already recognized as the preoccupation with presuppositions."[55] As an exemplar of this kink, R. G. Collingwood provides Hartt with an opportunity to consider the possibility of cultural transcendence in the theological critique of culture. Although Hartt probes Colling-

---

[53]For Hartt "common human experience" denotes the illusions of everyday life that must be exposed and criticized by the church's proclamation of the Gospel. See *CC*, 20-25.

[54]This is a very difficult matter to get clear, partly because our intellectual tradition and language continually betrays us. For a thorough and illuminating working over of these matters in a way with which I think Hartt would be deeply sympathetic, see Nicholas Lash, *Easter in Ordinary: Reflections on Human Experience and the Knowledge of God* (Charlottesville: University Press of Virginia, 1988).

[55]Ibid., 64.

wood's position for its coherence, his major concern is how this "preoccupation with presuppositions" has infected theology and deflected it from the claims of the Gospel. In his response Hartt does not delineate a method for his theology. Rather, he analyzes a cultural condition, shows how it is antithetical to the claims of the Gospel, and suggests how the Gospel can serve as the foundation of theology of culture.

Hartt takes Collingwood's notion of "absolute presuppositions" as an example of a view which "assumes a total lack of access to culture-transcending actuality." If one accepts Collingwood's notion, then

> the absolute foundation of every civilization is a value judgment which cannot be evaluated but must simply be taken for granted. Such a value is the absolute presupposition of a civilization. When such a value is finally exposed to evaluation, when it is vulnerable to criticism, it loses its absoluteness. When this has happened civilization has entered another epoch; or it has ceased altogether to exist as an effective synthesis of human interests and energies.[56]

Hartt identifies and rejects two ways theology has responded to this preoccupation with presuppositions.

One theological response claims that "faith in God revealed in Jesus Christ" is the presupposition of Christian criticism of culture, but sees that presupposition as simply the Christian instance of the peculiar and arbitrary presuppositions which people may hold—an instance of nonfoundationalism. On this view, since all presuppositions are arbitrary, Christian criticism has as much claim to validity as any other criticism, and more claim if good works commend Christian presuppositions.[57] But for Hartt such a relativist response

---

[56]Ibid., 67. For Collingwood's notion of "absolute presuppositions" see his *Essay on Metaphysics* (Oxford: Oxford University Press, 1940) chap. 5. For Hartt's thoroughgoing critique of Collingwood, see Julian N. Hartt, "Metaphysics, History, and Civilization: Collingwood's Account of Their Interrelationships," *Journal of Religion* 33 (1953): 198-211.

[57]Ibid., 66.

cannot sustain the preaching of the Gospel to the whole world which the Gospel itself demands.[58] Thus, the faithful church is driven on to seek another solution.

A second theological response celebrates the foundation of Western civilization in Christian values and obligates the Christian to accept and defend that civilization without extending the obligation any further.[59] Hartt rejects this response for its denial of any access to transcendent criticism of culture and for its consequent denial of "the persistence in [Western civilization] of the will to learn and obey the will of God who is infinitely more than the internal spirit of this civilization."[60] Ultimately, this position is historicist and denies the Gospel as the revelation of God and the human situation.

In his criticism of these responses Hartt accepts two assertions: (1) that Christian criticism derives from faith in God revealed in Jesus Christ, and (2) that we are "products" of civilization in the sense that "human possibility can be realized only in a society." But he goes beyond these to assert that "the demands of God revealed in Jesus Christ transcend every value system" and that a human being "comes to be a person in a pattern of relationships itself personal, that is, in a community not created by nor limited to any concrete social order."[61] These assertions again anticipate theological convictions about the Gospel, church, and world which we will explore in the following chapters. But we may note here Hartt's concern continually to guard the Gospel from any tendency toward ideality, toward its becoming the foundation of an ideology. The Gospel is the foundation of theology of culture, but

---

[58]Ibid. We will further consider Hartt's rejection of historical relativism in chap. 6.

[59]Though Hartt does not identify here a representative of this position, it sounds like Hartt's account of Emil Brunner's theology of culture, above.

[60]Ibid., 68.

[61]Ibid. Cf. *RQ*, 43: "Judgment upon and about the social order is inspired by its intuitions of the ground of human existence and of the world. This ground is revealed in Jesus Christ, 'through whom all things were made' (see John 1:3; Colossians 1:16) and 'in whom the fullness of God was pleased to dwell' (Col. 1:19)."

theology of culture is not the special pleading of one interest group, the church, within society; theology of culture is not the church's ideology. Rather, theology of culture is the church's response to the reality established and disclosed in the Gospel of Jesus Christ.

Hartt's answer to the possibility of a transcendent critique of culture supposes that the Gospel is the foundation of such critique. That answer is unsatisfactory to any foundationalist expectation of a less particular claim. Hartt's answer does not appeal to something already known apart from the Gospel. Rather, it demands conversion and consent to the Gospel. But Hartt's answer also runs contrary to the antifoundationalist acceptance of confessionalism and relativism. Since the Gospel reveals God and the human situation, an explication of the Gospel provides a way to assert its truth for all times and places. The authority of that demand and the credibility of the claim can only be displayed by an elucidation of the world according to the Gospel. Thus, we must now turn to Hartt's understanding of the Gospel as authority for theological critique of culture.

• Gospel as Authority •

When the church proclaims the good news that in Jesus Christ God has redeemed the world, the question often comes back, from both inside and outside the church, by what authority do you proclaim that redemption? This question asks for reasons, warrants, supports for the claim of the Gospel. As the question of authority has been variously construed and analyzed throughout the history of theology, it turns out not to be one question or problem but several: the problem of biblical authority, of ecclesiastical authority, of heteronomy versus autonomy, and various other construals.[62]

---

[62]One of the best theological analyses of authority is the brief but perceptive treatment by Nicholas Lash, *Voices of Authority* (Shepherdstown WV: Patmos Press, 1976).

With the recognition of the situatedness of theology, the question of authority has become even more acute. For foundationalists, their work is authorized by their chosen foundation. But the question then arises, how does a "foundation" in universal reason, common human experience, or a metaphysical scheme then authorize the particular claims of the Gospel? When the force of this dilemma turns theologians to antifoundationalism, the question then arises, how do you avoid a relativist and confessionalist theology? Are we confined to responding to challenges from other views by simply repeating, "because the Bible tells me so," or "because that is what Christians believe"?

Hartt certainly believes that Christians should be committed to making a case for their claims about the Gospel. He persistently argues that theological statements are assertions, not confessions.[63] So, with Hartt's recognition of the situatedness of theology and his conviction that the Gospel, in its particularity, is revelation and foundation for theology of culture, we must now turn to his account of how the Gospel authorizes "real and decisive case making." In forging an answer to these questions from Hartt's theology, we may once again see the force of his claim that the Gospel reveals God *and the human situation*.

Hartt's approach to Gospel and authority takes the problem of heteronomy versus autonomy as central, but in the process of analysis broadens the question and transforms the problem. After examining Hartt's analysis, we will locate him in relation to other contemporary construals of the authority of the Gospel.

Hartt's Analysis of Authority. Hartt provides a subtle and allusive analysis of authority in Chapter Five of *Theological Method and Imagination*.[64] Although Hartt advertises the chapter as a discussion of biblical authority, "Sola Scriptura: Problems about Authority," he considers a whole range of issues in a fruitful discussion of heteronomy versus autonomy. For theology, the distinction between heteronomy and autonomy identifies a dilemma. If the

---

[63]See *RQ*, 14-15; *TMI*, xiv. One of the major concerns of the latter work is delineating a theological approach to "real and decisive case making" (254).

[64]"Sola Scriptura: Problems about Authority," *TMI*, 108-33.

church appeals to autonomy, to warrants which are a part of the questioner's world, then how can its message be news, how can it be revelation, how can it be Gospel? If the church appeals to heteronomy, to warrants which are not a part of the questioner's world, then how can its message be good, how can it be Gospel?

Hartt uncovers the characteristics and the problems of heteronomy and autonomy, while also discerning the dynamics involved in the turn from heteronomy to autonomy.[65] In keeping with his theology of culture, he also uncovers the illusions present in each position, attending most closely to the illusions of autonomy. Hartt's own proposal rests on three concepts: a distinction between heteronomy and externality, God's asking for human consent, and God's desire for communion with humanity.

Hartt acknowledges that "it is very generally supposed in modern Christian theology that *heteronomy* and *externality*, in respect to authority, are interchangeable concepts."[66] But Hartt dismantles this supposition with a series of characterizations, questions, and counterproposals. For Hartt "the proper force of heteronomy is being subject to determination and thus domination by the will of another; that will being governed, so to speak, by either secret or unintelligible motives."[67]

According to Hartt the Christian God does not fit this description of heteronomy. Rather "the Other is a being altogether righteous, wise, and resourceful, so that he purely wills my good as he wills differentially the good of all."[68] Thus, although God revealed in the Gospel is external, is "other" in so far as God's will and God's commands are not to be assimilated or confused with one's own, God is not "an alien power. If it so appears, it is

---

[65]For a perceptive history of this quest for autonomy, see Jeffrey Stout, *The Flight from Authority: Religion, Morality and the Quest for Autonomy* (Notre Dame IN: University of Notre Dame Press, 1981).

[66]Hartt, *TMI*, 129.

[67]Ibid. In this critique he anticipates the approach of Lash, *Voices of Authority*, esp. chaps. 1 and 8.

[68]Ibid., 130. Hartt addresses the objections of theological determinists throughout his work. See, e.g., *TMI*, 126-28, and *CC*, 130-31, regarding the causality of preaching and election.

because the human citadel is now occupied by the spirit of alienation."[69] The flight from God as external authority, then, derives from illusions about the human situation, and from lies about, and misconstruals of, the God of Jesus Christ.[70] As I noted earlier, here and elsewhere Hartt's methodological concerns are penetrated by substantive convictions in ways which call into question our fastidious intellectualism.

Hartt also carries on his argument with the heteronomy/autonomy disjunction in a discussion of consent. Even in the midst of assertions of God's sovereignty, God's inescapability, and God's perfection, our acknowledgement of God's authority is neither coerced nor determined. Rather "we are asked to *consent*, to extend credit, to [God]."[71] Such an understanding of God's authority undermines the supposition that external authority equals heteronomy.

Finally, in responding to theological determinists' objections to his account, Hartt observes

> that scriptural views of the relation of God's absolute sovereignty to human perception and decision do not fit neatly or easily into theories of absolute divine determinism. For what God demands ultimately of mankind is communion. "Demand" is surely an odd verb to associate with the supreme mode of spiritual unity. I do not say that scripture itself makes that conjunction. The picture is rather more like this: Communion is what God purposes in his commands, it is their intention. Therefore God intends that human beings should trust him. But trust cannot be coerced. If, therefore, we are to believe that God is the cause, pure and

---

[69]Ibid., 131.

[70]In connection with this discussion of heteronomy and externality, Hartt rejects as unrealistic the "fear of a specifically Christian heteronomy," particularly one which is hegemonic. He sees "biblicist Protestantism" as "nearer the pole of autonomy than it is to heteronomy" because it domesticates revelation, assimilates it to the illusions of Everyday such that "whatever shatters, or threatens to shatter the structures of Everyday are construed to be demonic rather than divine" (*TMI*, 132-33). Hartt also argues that most dangerous to us is the exercise of authority "largely in subliminal forms. . . . [which] are overwhelmingly secular" (*TMI*, 131).

[71]Hartt, *TMI*, 126.

simple, of our trust in him, shall we not also and simply believe that he attracts our trust rather than produces it?[72]

Interwoven with this emphasis on communion as God's purpose are Hartt's distinction between heteronomy and externality and his claim that we are asked to consent to God's authority. Each of these aspects of Hartt's discussion is supported and developed by the others. Together they suggest that in Jesus Christ we find "a realm in which power and authority are perfectly united. What rules there is fit to rule, and is so honored by common judgment and consent. There authority is not won or sustained by deceit or coercion."[73]

In this construal of the authority of the Gospel, Hartt draws upon his understanding of the Gospel as revelation of God and the human situation. The Gospel is not simply a claim about God, which the church then imposes upon the world. Nor is the Gospel a claim about God, which is then authorized by showing how it agrees with some other account of human reason or experience. At the same time, the Gospel is not simply a claim about the human situation, which the church presents as something already known by the world through some other means. Rather, the Gospel is God's revelation of Godself and of the shape of the real world, that is, of the human situation. When we add to this the Gospel's claim that the real shape of the world is its creation and redemption (to be examined in the next chapter) by God, then the revelation of the Gospel is news, and it is good. It is news—it is something we would not know apart from the Gospel; and it is good—it is an invitation not to abandon our humanity, but to its redemption by

---

[72]Ibid., 127.

[73]Hartt, *TMI*, 126. Hartt introduces this as "one of the fondest dreams of humankind." As should be clear from other aspects of his thought which are displayed in this book, he does not mean by that phrase to suggest that Christianity is a projection.

our Creator.[74] Thus the authority of the Gospel which reveals God and the human situation is external, but it is not heteronomous.[75]

Locating Hartt. Bruce Marshall introduces *Christology in Conflict,* his study of the Christologies of Rahner and Barth, by sketching four approaches to "showing how Jesus Christ, the particular person whose identity is depicted in the Gospel stories, can be ultimately meaningful or significant."[76] Although Marshall moves in and out of the language of authority, his sketch is concerned with how theology authorizes Christological assertions. Therefore, it provides a map for locating Hartt's understanding of the Gospel as authority. Moreover, although his construal of Barth is similar to my construal of Hartt, the differences between them are even more instructive. So after relating Hartt to Marshall's four approaches, I will suggest that Hartt provides an approach superior to that which Marshall ascribes to Barth.

One approach to authority and the Gospel simply asserts biblical or divine authority as the warrant for the Gospel's claims. These assertions may be further buttressed by, for example, an appeal to evidentialist apologetics or ecclesiastical dogma—in which case do we have a simple assertion of biblical or divine authority? Or the assertion of biblical and divine authority may be cheerfully accepted as an inescapable fideism. A second approach

---

[74]For a similar approach, see Lash, *Voices,* 114. In a paraphrase of Rahner, he says that Christianity "commands [man] to fulfil himself, and charges man with himself, that is himself as the 'possibility of truth' in the acceptance of the truth in which God does not express something but expresses himself" (Lash, *Voices,* 114).

[75]In this section we have seen how the Gospel will serve as authority in Hartt's theology. Hartt's assertions about the authority of the Gospel rest upon his interpretation of the Gospel which we will examine in the next chapter. In other words, Hartt has shown how the authority of the Gospel might be established, but he has not yet established it. Such work is not the province of methodological reflection, but of theological interpretation. For that we will turn, in the next chapter to Hartt's earlier work, in particular the central section of *CC.*

[76]Bruce D. Marshall, *Christology in Conflict: The Identity of a Saviour in Rahner and Barth* (Oxford: Basil Blackwell, 1987) 1. The four approaches are delineated on 1-14.

to authority and the Gospel vests authority in some worldview, some supposed mind of the age, or some account of rationality, any one of which becomes the source of the criteria, the authority, by which the Gospel is judged. In this approach the Gospel can be proclaimed with no logically necessary connection to Jesus Christ. These first two approaches represent, ideally, the poles of heteronomy and autonomy in authority.[77]

A third approach seeks to mediate between the previous two approaches. This approach, says Marshall, distinguishes

> between two main tasks or questions in Christology. One task is to show how the kinds of significance Christians ascribe to Jesus Christ can be universally meaningful and accessible on the strength of their coherence with logically general criteria, which indicate what kind of thing can count as "ultimately meaningful" (such criteria often taking the form of a prethematic experience or structure putatively common to all persons). The complementary task is to explicate (rather than to establish or prove) the basic conviction that Jesus Christ is the particular person to whom alone these various kinds of significance actually belong.[78]

Marshall takes Rahner's Christology as an example of this mediating approach and shows that it cannot be consistently carried out. One can either appeal to logically general criteria, thus denying the particularity of Jesus Christ as Saviour, or one can retain the assertion of the particularity of Jesus Christ, thus excluding any appeal to logically general criteria.[79]

Marshall concludes that "because intrinsic logical barriers keep [the mediating approach] from being executed consistently, then contemporary Christology seems faced with an explicit choice about its basic aims."[80] The choice, he says, is between the "radical

---

[77]However, some caution must be exercised—cf. Hartt's description of biblicist protestantism as an expression of autonomy, above.

[78]Marshall, *Christology in Conflict*, 9.

[79]Ibid., 106.

[80]Ibid., 10.

revisionists" of the second approach described above and a fourth approach.

Marshall takes Barth as an example of this fourth approach. Barth, he argues, wants to avoid the first two approaches, not by mediating between them but by setting "the issue of the relation between Jesus' particularity and his significance on a basically different footing."[81] This approach seeks ways of

> articulating the conviction that Jesus Christ uniquely has the function of "that which is ultimately significant" in which the meaningfulness of this conviction does not depend upon an appeal to general, putatively universal criteria, but which do not on that account attempt to ground the meaningfulness of the conviction in an appeal to sheer divine authority.[82]

In this approach the particular identity of Jesus Christ is logically indispensable and materially decisive for claims about his ultimate significance.[83] Thus, the warrant for assertions about Jesus as redeemer is the demonstration that the particular identity of Jesus Christ is logically indispensable to the assertion, that the assertion has a "descriptive aptness," and that it has "the force of 'logically individuating' characterizations."[84] In Marshall's judgment, Barth answers the question of Jesus Christ's *heilsbedeutsam* in a way that "is both internally coherent and consistent with the assumption that only Jesus Christ, this particular person, is ultimately *heilsbedeutsam*."[85] But Marshall also notes an uneasiness that may attend Barth's account, since his way of honoring the particularity of Jesus Christ makes Jesus the criterion of significance for salvation. Is this any improvement on appeal to sheer divine authority?

---

[81]Ibid., 11.

[82]Marshall, *Christology in Conflict*, 11. I do not want to discard the possibility of an appeal to "sheer divine authority" as summarily as Marshall does, though I do agree that it is an impoverished position and no real solution.

[83]Marshall, *Christology in Conflict*, 134-43.

[84]Ibid., esp, 138-40. For Marshall's use of "Jesus Christ as a particular person" see 12, 42-47, 124-25.

[85]Ibid., 145.

Hartt closely resembles Marshall's fourth approach. For Hartt the authority of the Gospel cannot be established apart from explication of the Gospel. To attempt the former apart from the latter would require the importation of criteria alien to the Gospel. It would be to abandon the Gospel as foundation and as revelation, in effect, to preach another Gospel. So when Hartt analyzes "Sola Scriptura: Problems About Authority" in *Theological Method and Imagination,* he rehearses the practical and historical nature of the problems arising often as supposedly discrete methodological issues. But when he seeks to resolve the problems, he draws on his interpretation of the Gospel, alluded to and applied in *Theological Method and Imagination* and explicated most fully in *A Christian Critique of American Culture.*[86] Since Hartt's resolution of the methodological problems of authority derives from a posited understanding of the Gospel, he does not fall into the error of Marshall's third approach.

Thus, Hartt's approach to the authority of the Gospel resembles Marshall's fourth approach, but it also diverges from it. Marshall's fourth approach assimilates the problem of authority to the problem of meaningfulness and in so doing confines the problem to an internal affair for Christianity. Marshall shows how to make Christological assertions internally coherent and consistent, but on his account no further claims can be made.

Hartt cannot confine the problem in this way because of his understanding of the Gospel and his consequent concern for theological critique of culture and for evangelism.[87] To put it briefly, Hartt is more willing to consider the concerns of what has traditionally been labeled apologetic theology, but he is not willing to

---

[86]In his "Introduction" Hartt warns us of the interpenetration of methodological issues and substantive convictions (*TMI,* xiv-xvi). Indeed, I will argue in this section that Hartt's discussion of authority in *TMI,* which has a methodological focus, and his "Christological" section in *CC,* which has a substantial focus, depend upon one another.

[87]This is not to say that Marshall or Marshall's Barth are unconcerned about such issues, but Marshall's explication of this fourth approach offers no direct support for such tasks.

do so at the expense of the Gospel, the *kerygma*.[88] In this he shares the concerns of Marshall's interpretation of Barth. But he combines *kerygmatic* conviction with apologetic concern, not because the world demands it nor because the church desires acceptance, but because the Gospel requires it.[89] Whether Hartt successfully combines these concerns can only be judged by looking at his interpretation of the Gospel, which will be our topic in the next chapter.

• Conclusion •

Hartt's description of theology of culture as "interpretation of a system of values, creations, and attitudes in the light of and on the basis of the revelation of being and good in Jesus Christ" directs us to the roles of the Gospel that we have examined in this chapter.[90] The Gospel is "the revelation of being and good in Jesus Christ." The "light of" the Gospel identifies its role as revelation, disclosing God and the human situation. "On the basis of" the Gospel identifies its role as the foundation of theology of culture, displacing all other possible foundations. Although it is not explicitly stated in this quote, the Gospel as authority for theology of culture clearly follows from its role as revelation and as foundation.

In these three roles of the Gospel, we have a further understanding of Hartt in relation to other theologies of culture.[91] In his

---

[88]Cf. *CC*, 75-76: "I contend that the rejection of apologetics is itself an error. The rejection of apologetics is very likely to convert the purity of Biblical faith into an ideal which cannot be compromised because it cannot be realized. But the rejection of apologetics is itself to be rejected for a more serious reason. It makes an adequate interpretation of the dialectic of the Kingdom of God impossible. Without that dialectic the world of divine creation and of divine redemption splits into two unreal and mutually hostile parts."

[89]See our further consideration of apologetic and *kerygmatic* approaches in chap. 5.

[90]*RQ*, 49.

[91]In this and the following two paragraphs, comparisons between Hartt and specific theologians could be endlessly multiplied and debated. I have chosen to leave the discussion at a more general level, partly in deference to Hartt's own practice and partly out of a desire to keep the focus on Hartt.

understanding of the Gospel as revelation of God and the human situation, Hartt distances his work from two theological approaches. On the one hand, some, treating the Gospel as solely the revelation of God, either end up with a kind of confessionalism or look outside the Gospel to some other account of the human situation in order to interpret the Gospel. In contrast, Hartt treats the claims of the Gospel about God as tied to claims about the human situation. If the Gospel's claims about the human situation are shown to be true, then its claims about God are also true.[92] On the other hand, some, treating the Gospel solely as a claim about the human situation, feel free to revise the claims of the Gospel in the light of changing cultural and religious understandings of the human situation. In contrast, Hartt treats the claims of the Gospel about the human situation as tied to claims about God. That is, the Gospel is God's revelation of the human situation, not human construction of our situation then attributed to God. Therefore, Hartt looks to the Gospel for an account of the human situation which then becomes the basis for a critical interpretation of other accounts.

Thus, in his understanding of the Gospel as foundation, Hartt distances himself from two approaches. In contrast to those who think that theology can be done apart from constant attention to the cultural situation, Hartt argues that theology from beginning to end must be concerned with its cultural situation.[93] In contrast to those who view theology of culture as rooted in some pretheological analysis of culture as the basis of theological work, Hartt argues that a true understanding of our situation is founded in the Gospel's revelation.[94]

---

[92] I will develop this claim at several points, but see esp. chap. 6. In Hartt's work, see *TMI*, chaps. 1 and 2.

[93] *CC*, xviii, quoted above.

[94] See the carefully nuanced assertion: "Surely some presentiments of the one true God must be forthcoming in the creativity of culture, unless we imagine that God did not learn to speak until Moses appeared, who taught Him Hebrew. But the very minute cultural creativity is endowed with divine meaning the specter of idolatry moves front and center from the wings" (*CC*, 137).

Finally, then, in his understanding of the Gospel as authority, Hartt again distances himself from two approaches. First, in contrast to those who appeal to some criteria outside the Gospel as authorizing theology as cultural critique, Hartt, without arguing the incoherence of that approach at length, simply shows that if the Gospel reveals God and the human situation, then the only authority to which we may appeal is the Gospel. Secondly, in contrast to those who believe that such a construal of the Gospel's authority shuts one up to some kind of confessionalism, Hartt argues that the Gospel's revelation of the human situation provides a way to assert and not merely confess the truth of the Gospel.

Of course, these comparisons produce certain expectations of Hartt's theology and commit his theology to certain tasks. We expect him to show how, and not merely say that, the Gospel reveals God and the human situation. We expect his theology to expose the truths and illusions of our culture. Finally, we expect his theology to assert the truth of such claims and make a case for believing them. In other words, we expect from Hartt a theological critique of culture. To Hartt's fulfillment of his commitments and our expectations we now turn.

Chapter 3

The Re-Presentation
of the Gospel in
Hartt's Theology of Culture

> But first I must know who Jesus Christ is, I must learn why and
> how as a Christian I say that the criterion of all Christian witness,
> and therefore of every judgment of the world, is not so much a
> life as a living presence, and everlasting actuality. To be Christian
> is to surrender one's life to the interpretation of the Holy Spirit
> whose text is Jesus Christ. The Christian is not a mere passive
> object in this process. He too is a subject. He is an interpreter as
> well as an interpretation, he is a speaker as well as a word. He
> must know what to speak about Jesus Christ before he knows
> what to say about the good and evil of this world.[1]

As we have seen, Hartt recognizes the situatedness of theology
and calls theology to a critique of culture. In the previous chapter,
I argued that these characteristics of Hartt's theology are rooted in
his conviction that the Gospel is the revelation of God and the real
shape of the world, that the Gospel is the foundation of theological
interpretation of culture, and that the Gospel's authority combines
and corrects what may roughly be called apologetic and kerygmatic theology. Hartt's understanding of these three roles may be com-
mended, at this point, on grounds of their fruitfulness in resolving
methodological dilemmas. But on Hartt's own account the most

---

[1]CC, 119-20.

persuasive argument for them would be a re-presentation of the Gospel in which we are grasped by God and by the shape of the real world, the human situation, as it is revealed in the Gospel. The term "re-presentation" characterizes Hartt's theology, because what Hartt seeks is best described not as an interpretation of the Gospel for our times, but a critique of our culture by the Gospel. This is consistent with his claims about the Gospel as revelation, foundation and authority, and also, as we will see, with his claim that the Gospel is a present reality—in the words of the epigraph for this chapter, a "living presence, and everlasting actuality." That is, if the Gospel is a present reality, our primary responsibility is not to interpret the meaning of some past event for the present, but to discern that present reality and re-present it to others in such a way that they too discern it and participate in it. So, although Hartt talks about "interpreting" the Gospel, his use of the phrase must be understood within the context of his theology. "Re-presentation" rather than "interpretation" best conveys Hartt's practice.

In this chapter, then, we will examine Hartt's presentation of the Gospel in the light of his claims about theology as cultural critique and the roles of the Gospel in that theology. In order to prepare for understanding Hartt's work, we must recognize that Hartt's presentation of the Gospel is very much like a sermon. His elevation of practical theology and preachability, noted in the previous chapter, already signal this characteristic. Another indication is Hartt's narrowing of the gap between "systematics" and homiletics.[2] For Hartt this movement depends upon a shift in perceiving theology more as an artistic than a scientific endeavor (though he recognizes that science is also something of an art form). In this conception of theology, concerns traditionally ascribed to aesthetics receive more notice.[3]

In this turn to aesthetics, criteria for judging theology emerge in addition to, but not in competition with, the criterion of preach-

---

[2]Hartt, "Fall-out from Shifts in the Winds of Doctrine," 36-38.

[3]Hartt's essay "Fall-out from Shifts in the Winds of Doctrine" is a consideration of the place of arts in theological education.

ability. In *Theological Method and Imagination*, Hartt considers relevancy, consistency, congruency and fertility as criteria, while in "Fall-out" he accentuates coherence-and-clarity, vividness, and engagement.[4] Although the first list is applied to theology and the second to the sermon, both express the same concerns. Relevancy is related to and disciplined by preachability. One expression of the properly disciplined quest for relevance is vividness, the use of captivating metaphors and powerful rhetoric. Consistency (= coherence-and-clarity) means that one should not frustrate readers by claiming one thing and also its contradiction. Aesthetic coherence and consistency, however, is not the same as logical consistency.[5] Aesthetic coherence can tolerate, indeed thrives on, tension and dissonance, while formal, logical consistency must resolve such elements. Congruency calls for engagement with the actualities of a situation in such a way that the imagination is engaged and commitment is enabled. In the context of theology, fertility enforces a practical concern not unlike the homiletical concern for commitment. The criterion of fertility asks if the theology under review enables the Christian and the church to get on with the work of the Gospel.

Since Hartt's theology follows these criteria, his presentation of the Gospel is like a sermon. His work seeks aesthetic coherence, vividness, engagement and fertility. Therefore, he does not argue exegetically or historically for his presentation of the Gospel. Rather, he seeks to present the Gospel in such a way as to allow readers to discover themselves in it. Thus, theology of culture, as the interpretation of values, dispositions, and creations in the light

---

[4]*TMI*, 70-74; "Fall-out," 30-32. See also Hartt's consideration of aesthetic truthfulness in Julian Hartt, "Theological Investments in Story: Some Comments on Recent Developments and Some Proposals," with replies from Stephen Crites and Stanley Hauerwas, and a reply to them from Hartt, *Journal of the American Academy of Religion* 52 (March 1984): 117-56, and his application of the criterion of fertility to the work of Karl Barth in David L. Dickerman, *Karl Barth and the Future of Theology*, A Memorial Colloquium Held at the Yale Divinity School, 28 January 1969 (New Haven CT: Yale Divinity School Association, 1969) 42-44.

[5]"Fall-out," 30-31, *TMI*, 70. See Hartt's remarks on formal consistency as at best a secondary virtue in Dickerman, *Karl Barth and the Future of Theology*, 42.

of the Gospel, seeks to represent God and the human situation in such a way that the reader responds and participates in the Gospel.

Such theology is not supported by exegetical or historical-critical arguments.[6] An appeal to criteria appropriate to those modes of argument, or any criteria other than those specified above, would effectively work against Hartt's theology by undermining it. In other words, one would deny what one set out to recommend if one were to adduce arguments for Hartt's theology on the basis of exegetical accuracy, historiography, a metaphysical scheme, or an account of the religious dimension in human experience. Hartt's theology is biblical in that it seeks to present the vision of reality established and revealed in the biblical witness to Jesus Christ, but it is not biblicist in that claims for the truth of the Gospel are not based on "because the Bible tells me so," but on the persuasiveness of the Gospel's claims about the real shape of the world and the human situation.

Thus, in order to persuade someone of the rightness of Hartt's theology, one can only present Hartt's theology and show that it fits the appropriate criteria. Such an approach is open-ended. It is also pluralistic in the sense that there is no one way by which people come to be persuaded of the Gospel. It allows each reader to find himself or herself, or perhaps better, to be found, at any point in a presentation of the Gospel. Such an approach is also expansive—it takes time to unfold. Finally, Hartt's approach is complex. It does not move from what the Gospel meant to what it means, nor does it move from the meaning of the Gospel to its application. All of these are bound up together so tightly that any attempt to separate them falters, due not only to the complexity of

---

[6]This is not to deny a certain kind of dependence on exegesis and historical criticism. Since Hartt's theology continues to be informed by the Bible he is dependent in some ways upon the work of grammarians, linguists, and historians. However, their work is the ground, not the warrant for his theological arguments. To this relationship must be added his transformation of history, below.

the task but also due to its betrayal of the basic premise of Hartt's theology.[7]

David Kelsey describes Hartt's presentation of the Gospel as "a powerfully written, imaginatively original, and largely ignored christological essay. . . . "[8] In this chapter I could fully communicate the power, originality, and persuasiveness of Hartt's account only by reproducing his entire essay. In this case, my secondary account of Hartt's work will be less persuasive than the primary text. Nonetheless, in this chapter I will present a synopsis of Hartt's presentation of the Gospel in order to promote further attention to Hartt's work and set some parameters for its interpretation and appropriation.

Hartt introduces his presentation of the Gospel with the assertion that "Christian faith incorporates things known and things believed. The ontological fundamentals of man's being are things known. Chief among the things believed is: the scriptural witness to Jesus Christ is true."[9] From this assertion he derives the theological task, which is "to show how the things believed do in fact grapple with the ontological fundamentals of the human condition."[10] Since "ontological fundamentals" sounds like an appeal to something other than the Gospel, an approach which I have argued that Hartt rejects, I will take a close look at how he uses the concept. Here I want simply to disarm any immediate rejection of my interpretation of Hartt's work. Later we will consider the reasons for the Hartt's persistent use of "ontology."

---

[7]Thus, Hartt agrees with Frei and others that the meaning of the Gospel is the Gospel. But by recognizing that the Gospel itself makes claims about the human situation, and especially by making that recognition a central element in his theology, Hartt goes beyond Frei and others. We will return to this point in chap. 6.

[8]David Kelsey, "Christian Sense Making: Hartt's *Theological Method and Imagination*," *Journal of Religion* 58 (1978): 435.

[9]Hartt, CC, 164.

[10]Ibid.

• Ontological Fundamentals •

Hartt scatters throughout his work talk about the ontological fundamentals, the ontological essentials, the fundamental realities and concrete actualities of human existence. Initially these terms refer to the same five elements: death, love, creativity, anxiety, and guilt.[11] Hartt says that "a civilization is (and not just offers) a particular interpretation of the ontological essentials."[12] But he also claims that "each of them has its own brute reality. None of them is really mastered by civilization."[13]

An unfavorable reading of Hartt's use of "ontological fundamentals" could claim a contradiction in Hartt's theology so basic that his work is rendered inept. How does one assert the "brute reality" of the fundamentals as though that reality, or that claim of brute reality, were not itself dependent upon a particular interpretation rendered by a civilization? When Hartt appears to give a brief account of the brute reality of the ontological fundamentals, is he not simply wrong on his own account, or at least my interpretation of it?[14] Has he not introduced a conception in total opposition to his basic perspective? In contrast, a more favorable reading of "brute reality" could draw on his claim that at some level we must reckon *with a world imposed, not a world created.*[15] On this reading "brute reality" is not an epistemological or metaphysical doctrine which opposes or stands independent from the Gospel; rather, "brute reality" is a particular culture's construal of the real shape of the world, the human situation, which is the

---

[11]The first occurrence of these terms in *CC* is on 70. But cf. the less schematized account in *TTE*, 42-59. In other sections of *CC*, the ontological essentials of the human situation are described in other terms. See below, 65-74.

[12]Ibid., 71.

[13]Ibid., 70.

[14]Ibid., 70-71. Hartt does not explicitly claim to be giving an account of the brute reality of the fundamentals, but that seems to be implied.

[15]Julian Hartt, "Theological Investments in Story: Some Comments on Recent Developments and Some Proposals," *Journal of the American Academy of Religion* 52 (Winter 1984): 125-26.

subject of a theological critique that discerns the Gospel at work in human culture.

Hartt's talk about ontological fundamentals derives from his claim that Jesus Christ "came into a human world, not into a howling unbroken wilderness."[16] Thus

> we have to admit not only that there are things we know about being and human being apart from Jesus Christ, but also that some of these things are essential for the right interpretation of the knowledge we have in Jesus Christ. Not to admit these things, or to refuse to develop them, is to make the wrong assertion of the absoluteness of Jesus Christ. The mysteries of being and human existence are not silenced or cleared up by shouting "Jesus Christ" as loudly as possible.[17]

This concern enters into Hartt's criticism of Barth's claim "that man does not know what sin is apart from Jesus Christ." Hartt says:

> This is rather like saying that people don't really know what suffering and death are apart from textbooks in pathology and rites for the dead; unless Barth intends only to say that we faithful Christians *really* know how to use the word "sin." I do not suppose that Barth meant to deny that other people know anything about moral conflict, guilt, the fatal loss of self-respect, and kindred phenomena.[18]

Hartt softens his critique and clarifies his position when he states that knowing the ontological essentials "does not mean that we know adequately what we need to be saved from (or what questions to ask) before we lay hold of salvation."[19]

In these passages Hartt reveals four uses of the concept of ontological fundamentals. First, "ontological fundamentals" acknowledges one import of the Incarnation: that Jesus Christ came into a

---

[16]Ibid., 72.
[17]Ibid., 70.
[18]Hartt, *TMI*, 240.
[19]Ibid., 70.

"world" made by humanity. Secondly, theology also must reckon with "worlds" already made by humanity.[20] Thirdly, only in Jesus Christ do we learn to see rightly the human situation and to act rightly in it: "the Christian claim is that the power and purpose Jesus Christ reveals in the reconstitution of human existence are precisely the power and purpose by which human existence is originally constituted."[21] Fourthly, human being must reckon with structures, or contexts, imposed.[22] If these four affirmations are what Hartt means by ontological fundamentals, then he has not introduced into his theology an alien concept.

Further support for my contention can be found in what Hartt does not do with "ontological fundamentals." One thing he does not do is provide a metaphysical system or a full-blown ontology in support of his claims about the ontological fundamentals.[23] Hartt also does not use the "ontological fundamentals" in order to provide a developed anthropology, which then becomes the general criteria by which one measures Jesus' meaningfulness and authority.[24]

Hartt's use and nonuse of "ontological fundamentals," then, does not deny *a priori* his other theological commitments and

---

[20]I will examine Hartt's concept of "world" in chap. 5.

[21]Ibid., 72.

[22]See *TTE*, 43, where Hartt lists "the context of nature, the context of society, the context of community, the context of history," and notes that "ontology" is the classical term for such concerns.

[23]In chap. 6 I will further explore Hartt's re-placing of metaphysics and show that he is not susceptible to Hans Jonas's critique of the Christian appropriation of Heidegger found in Hans Jonas, *The Phenomenon of Life: Toward a Philosophical Biology* (New York: Harper & Row, 1963) 235-61. For now I can note that Hartt issues severe strictures against theology of culture which is concerned with the "metaphysical animal" (as in his description of Tillich's appropriation of ontology in a Heideggerian mode), in *CC*, 8-13; see also Hartt's Taylor lectures, where he severely criticizes Tillich's "onto-theology" for making all of the critical decisions on the basis of ontology, before getting to theology.

[24]The most prominent recent example of this approach is Karl Rahner, *Foundations of Christian Faith. An Introduction to the Idea of Christianity*, trans. William V. Dych (New York: Crossroad, 1987). See Marshall's explication and critique of Rahner in *Christology in Conflict*, 15-114.

convictions regarding the Gospel revealed in Jesus Christ. Rather, he subjects the ontological fundamentals to the discipline of the Gospel. That is, these "ontological fundamentals" are part of that system of "values, creations, and attitudes" that is to be interpreted "in the light of and on the basis of the revelation of being and good in Jesus Christ." Hartt's treatment of these ontological fundamentals in his presentation of the Gospel shows implicitly that the Gospel is in control of Hartt's account. To that presentation of the Gospel we now turn.

• The Gospel in the Preaching, Person, and Work of Jesus Christ •

All along the way that we have thus far travelled I have demonstrated Hartt's commitment to the Gospel and anticipated his elucidation of that Gospel. I have also argued that for Hartt presentation of the Gospel always involves critical interpretation of various competing construals of the human situation. In the central section of *A Christian Critique of American Culture*, Hartt offers an elucidation of the Gospel of Jesus Christ as "the dogmatic content of practical theology" and at the same time interprets critically various construals of our situation.[25]

In Hartt's three chapters on the Gospel in the preaching, person, and work of Jesus Christ, he is committed to holding together what has often been disjoined: "the word given to the church to proclaim," he says, "is at once a message concerning the Kingdom of God and an acknowledgment of a person."[26] According to Hartt this unity has often been sundered, the church taking responsibility for preaching the Kingdom, theologians taking responsibility for interpreting the Person. Theology, too, has often

---

[25]Ibid., 123-348, esp. 165-230.

[26]Hartt, *CC*, 165. Cf. *TTE*, 26: "In the New Testament this concrete historical actuality, Jesus Christ, is interpreted in three ways of primary importance for our reflection: Jesus Christ is the supreme witness to the kingdom of God; Jesus Christ is the incarnate Lord, the crown prince and heir of the Kingdom; Jesus Christ is the Kingdom."

sundered these two, one school preferring the preaching of Jesus, another, his person and work.

But sundering the Gospel in this way denies the very Gospel which is to be proclaimed. Therefore, in light of this sundering, "the first task of theology is to show how the Christ of the Gospel and the Gospel of Christ are to be preached as a unity created by God, a unity that man must not sunder."[27] Hartt has a large stake in displaying this unity since it coheres with and supports his claim that the revelation of God in Jesus Christ reveals, at the same time, God and the human situation.[28]

Hartt's presentation of the Gospel in the preaching, person, and work of Jesus Christ centers on the image of the Kingdom. Hartt begins with an elucidation of the qualities of the Kingdom which Jesus proclaimed. Then he shows that Jesus not only preached the Kingdom, he also embodied it. Finally, the chapter on the work of Jesus Christ shows that his death and resurrection are one with his identity in transforming the "generic elements" (ontological fundamentals) of the being of humanity and in establishing the Kingdom which he proclaimed.[29] Hartt separates the preaching, person, and work of Jesus Christ only to show that they are not bases for different Gospels; they are different aspects of the one Gospel—the Gospel of the Kingdom of God.

In Hartt's exposition of the Gospel, three aspects of the Kingdom stand out: its actuality, its intelligibility, and its dialectic of creation and redemption. These three aspects are not imposed by Hartt; they arise out of his interpretation. They do not control Hartt's exposition, nor do they exhaust its meaning. However, they do identify the pillars of his theology of culture. In order to resist the impression that Hartt brings these three characteristics to his

---

[27]Ibid., 166.

[28]See above, chap. 2, s.v. "The Gospel as Revelation."

[29]In *CC*, 210, Hartt enters a *caveat*: "Even though the theological distinction between the Person and the Work of Jesus Christ lends itself to artificial amplification and application, the abuses of the distinction must not blind us to its values. Properly drawn it reinforces the conviction that God acts in the work of Jesus Christ."

interpretation of the Gospel, I do not use them to organize my presentation of Hartt's interpretation of the Gospel. After the presentation we will attend more closely to them and relate them to his conception of theology as cultural critique.

The Preaching of Jesus Christ. According to Hartt, the Gospel of Jesus Christ, that is, what he preached, is the Kingdom of God. Hartt acknowledges that the dominant view holds that the Gospels, including the account of Jesus' preaching, are the creation of the church. But he qualifies this acknowledgment by asserting the theological claim that "the church of the New Testament epoch found in its mouth the thing Jesus Christ had given it to say."[30] And against the view that the New Testament includes "some incredible yarns," Hartt asserts that

> even the most incredible yarn in the New Testament (and we cheerfully permit the historian to take his pick) has a clarity, pertinency, and sobriety, relative to the Gospel Jesus Christ himself preaches, which make post-New Testament hagiolatry look like wildly hyperbolic, undisciplined and even morbid exercises of imagination. This suggests very strongly that the imaginations of the preachers of the New Testament were under a very powerful and sure-handed discipline; and I take it that this discipline is the Gospel Jesus Christ himself preached.[31]

These assertions by Hartt do not "prove" his position, but they do qualify the opposing positions in such a way that Hartt's exposition of Jesus' preaching of the Kingdom is not ruled out *a priori*.[32]

---

[30]Ibid., 166.

[31]Ibid., 167.

[32]Thomas Langford has pointed out to me that Hartt wrote at a time when Bultmann's rejection of the *Was* of Jesus Christ was still ascendant. One of the provocative elements in Hartt's work is that he does not engage the argument on historical-critical grounds. Rather, Hartt shows the mutual dependence and coherence of the preaching, person, and work of Jesus. In this he moves in the tradition of Martin Kähler, *The So-Called Historical Jesus and the Historic Biblical Christ*, trans. and ed. Carl E. Braaten, with a foreword by Paul Tillich and an introduction by Carl E. Braaten (Philadelphia: Fortress Press, 1964), though in a different way from Paul Tillich. For Tillich on history and theology, see David H.

Hartt considers five qualities of the Kingdom as proclaimed by Jesus. First, he elucidates the nearness of the Kingdom.[33] The nearness of the Kingdom, as its imminence, "pins down the meaning, terrible and wonderful, of the present moment; but it does not tell us what the Kingdom is."[34] To stop at this point with the nearness of the Kingdom would be to establish its importance but evacuate its content; it would be to assert the value of religious experience but empty it of knowledge. However, the nearness of the Kingdom also asserts its likeness to human arrangements, "it is near in its perfect recognizability."[35] Thus, although the Kingdom is not a human creation, it is a human community, really the only human community. For Hartt, the proper way to think of this is not analogy because (1) analogy limits the freedom of God and (2) "the business of analogy misses the essential point in the New Testament similitudes of the Kingdom, namely, that Jesus Christ so sharply and decisively delineates its quality and shape that a man is left without excuse when he is asked why he has not chosen the Kingdom."[36] Finally, the nearness of the Kingdom intends the

---

Kelsey, *The Fabric of Paul Tillich's Theology*, Yale Publications in Religion, 13 (New Haven: Yale University Press, 1967) chap. 4, and D. Moody Smith, Jr., "The Historical Jesus in Paul Tillich's Christology," *Journal of Religion* 46 (January 1966): 131-47. For Hartt, see chap. 6, below.

[33]Ibid., 167-71.
[34]Ibid., 168.
[35]Ibid., 169.
[36]Ibid., 170. Hartt continues his critique:

Standing at a spiritual distance created in part by theologians, we can easily and lightheartedly decide that "father," "judge," and "lord" (and all other titles and attributes of God) are symbols; and thereafter gather information to decide whether they are living or dead symbols. In this way theologians become amateur sociologists rather than subtle philosophers. But the moral is about the same: One must wait upon an expert decision about religious language before one can become a real Christian.

I agree with Hartt's polemic. However, given Hartt's understanding of dogma as a human device, his constructive purposes might be better served by approaching analogy in a way similar to the distinction between the *modus significandi* and the *significatum*, as drawn from Thomas by George Lindbeck, in *The Nature of*

certainty of its truthfulness as the fulfillment of the promise that the plan of creation will be perfected and as the revelation that humanity must repent of humanity's membership in a counterfeit kingdom in order to enter the Kingdom of God.[37]

The second quality of the Kingdom delineated by Hartt is its dearness. The Kingdom has supreme value "as the fulfillment of a promise so time binding and historically essential as to be fundamental in man's being."[38] This value does not derive from human expectation or aspiration; rather, the Kingdom grounds human existence, "draws aspiration to it, and . . . disciplines expectation."[39] Thus, the Kingdom is news, but it is news that reveals longings, created by God, which humanity has perverted and can know again only by God's actuality; and, therefore, it is news which affirms humanity. But because of this value and source, the Kingdom can be had only through obedience, it cannot be mastered or replicated.[40]

The Kingdom is also dear in its costliness to those who would enter it: "the Kingdom demands everything."[41] Although the Kingdom demands the simplification of existence, that simplification does not call for the despisement or denial of this world, because

---

Doctrine, 66-69, and David Burrell, in *Aquinas: God and Action* (Notre Dame IN: University of Notre Dame Press, 1979).

[37]Throughout his exposition Hartt alternates between "man" referring to an individual, i.e., "a man," and "man" referring to collective humanity. I have not been able to discern anything systematic or significant in this alternation. Perhaps the alternation is itself systematic and significant, displaying Hartt's intention to avoid individualism and collectivism.

[38]Ibid., 171.

[39]Ibid., 172.

[40]Ibid., 171-72. Hartt's strictures against world mastery recall his description of Richard Kroner's theology of culture, above, 9-10. "Replicated" is my substitute for what Hartt describes as "successfully" or "effectively" counterfeited. There are two problems with Hartt's terms. First, he admits that the Kingdom has been counterfeited. Secondly, as ordinary usage goes he would also have to admit that some counterfeits of the Kingdom are "successful" as counterfeits, since many accept one or another counterfeit as the real thing and refuse to surrender that illusion. I think "replicate" better expresses what he is getting at.

[41]Ibid., 173.

the Kingdom is God fulfilling the plan of creation. Neither can simplification "be systematized as a social program," because the Kingdom is not the ideality of a program but the actuality of God.[42] Finally, the costliness of the Kingdom for those who would enter it means that "being already assured of God's acceptance, the Christian accepts his cross as part of his total obedience."[43]

The third quality of the Kingdom is its "perfection of the plan of creation."[44] As this perfection the Kingdom exposes our perversions of humanity's created potential and restores true joy and peace. In the Gospel of Jesus Christ the joy and peace of the Kingdom of God are "even now made available to those who believe in Him."[45] Hartt's exposition seeks to relate joy and peace rightly to the Kingdom which is the fulfillment of the world. Joy and peace are affective correlates of the Kingdom which is free and everlasting and the fulfillment of the plan of creation.

The fourth quality of the Kingdom is the perfection of its unity. Because of the plenitude of God's own life present in the Kingdom, we can each become fully what we are meant to be without diminishing one another. Unity is achieved without destroying individuality. We can lose our own lives and find them in the Kingdom which is God's life. We can be ourselves in all our particularity without diminishing the community. This perfection means that "no existing human organization is the model actualization of the Gospel. Every empirical human community excludes or downgrades some elements of mankind."[46]

The fifth quality of the Kingdom is really an answer to the question of who is in the Kingdom. Hartt says that membership in the Kingdom extends to all who accept and obey its law. Hartt

---

[42]Here Hartt signals his critique of the Social Gospel (*CC*, 3-4, 14-15) and of "revolutionary theology" (*CC*, 410-25, *TTE*, 76-87). See my discussion of this critique in chap. 5.

[43]Ibid., 176.

[44]Ibid., 176.

[45]Ibid.

[46]Ibid., 180. This assertion will be significant in our discussion, in chap. 4, of the relationship between the kingdom and the church.

argues that this answer dispenses with distinctions between repentance, faith in Jesus Christ, and obedience to his teachings. First, Jesus Christ's preaching of repentance does not mean "that the hearer of the Gospel already knows all that he needs to know about the law of the Kingdom."[47] Nor does it mean that the law of the Kingdom can be deduced from the law of the Old Testament or from humankind's moral sense. Rather, "the demand of repentance is a demand that the hearer desist from doing hateful things and begin doing the things in which love is expressed."[48] For Hartt, *love* is the law (which is not a law) of the Kingdom. The works of love express one's acceptance of and obedience to the Kingdom as

> a response to the righteousness of the Kingdom of God, disclosed in the mighty deeds of Jesus Christ, those good works of his that are the only authentic "signs and wonders" of the Kingdom of God in history, that same Jesus Christ who went about doing good, and who in the perfection of love was obedient even unto death upon the cross.[49]

Hartt has now brought us back to his purpose, to showing "the confluence of Christ's preaching of the Kingdom and the presence of the Kingdom in his own person."[50] The faith that makes us a part of the Kingdom is obedience to Jesus Christ. The first disciples of Jesus "did not begin by sharing his knowledge of the Kingdom but by obeying his representations of its reality and of its demands upon them."[51] We can learn from the knowledge which they acquired, "but the demands of the Kingdom are exactly the same. For us as for them Jesus Christ is the author and pioneer of our faith and of our salvation."[52] The Kingdom is not an ideal which

---

[47]Ibid., 181.
[48]Ibid., 183.
[49]Ibid., 183.
[50]Ibid.
[51]Ibid., 184.
[52]Ibid.

is merely known; the Kingdom is an actuality which is something to be seen and something to be done.

In these five qualities of the Kingdom Hartt has elucidated the Gospel preached by Jesus Christ. By his own claim of the confluence of the Kingdom in Jesus' preaching, person, and work, Hartt must now show how this preaching of Jesus Christ and the person of Jesus Christ form a unity created by God.

The Person of Jesus Christ. In his chapter on "The Identity of Christ the Preacher," Hartt wrestles with two issues. First, as I have already noted, Hartt acknowledges that, because of the claim that Jesus is a historical novelty, the question of Jesus' authority merges with the question of his identity.[53] Secondly, Hartt recognizes that when the questions of authority and identity merge, the answer to the questions cannot be based on speculative metaphysics.[54] To seek for such a basis would be to appeal to another authority beside the Gospel. But at the same time Hartt does not assert sheer divine or biblical authority. Therefore, Hartt contends that the question of Jesus' authority and identity can only be answered in relation to "a nonspeculative metaphysical account of man's being."[55]

Therefore, in this chapter Hartt displays the ontological ground of Jesus' authority and identity: "[Jesus Christ] is what he is from

---

[53]Ibid., 186-87.

[54]In chap. 6 I will examine the place of metaphysics in Hartt's theology. For now see Hartt, CC, 187: "Drawing upon the speculative resources of pagan culture the church very early began to crystallize its confession as metaphysical doctrines of the relationship of the Father to the Son. Throughout the Christian centuries the church has tried valiantly to preach these doctrines; and even now the creedal churches appeal to them as to the rule of faith. I believe this courage is misplaced and for a categorically simple reason: The speculative mode has its own reward and it can neither be packaged for general distribution in an era nor bound upon the spirits of souls yet unborn as the content of their good faith." As we will see Hartt allows for metaphysics, but not as the foundation of Christian theology.

[55]Hartt, CC, 187 passim. Hartt refers back to the chapter which identified the ontological fundamentals of human existence. However, as we shall see, in this chapter he uses different terms. He picks up the ontological fundamentals in the next chapter.

the depths of his being. He says what he says because of his command of the elemental powers of human being."[56] But he displays Jesus Christ's command of these powers apart from any appeal to metaphysics in the philosophical or the theological tradition. Hartt contrasts the ontological ground of Christ's authority to "characterological" and "moral" grounds. An appeal on characterological grounds is mistaken, because Jesus can appear to be an authoritarian personality or a deluded megalomaniac. An appeal to his moral attributes is mistaken because they are the expressions of, not the ground of, his authority:

> He was not called Son of God because he was a good man. His goodness expresses his Sonship and Lordship. In his full humanity Jesus Christ is in full command of the fundamental realities of man's being. He is in the human situation and in human life to the lowermost levels. But he is in the depths of human being as one from on high. His participation in human being is the participation of God.[57]

By showing how Jesus takes up into his own being the word which the Gospel addresses to "the concrete actualities of the human condition," Hartt adds, to his earlier exposition of the Gospel which Jesus preached, the claim that Jesus Christ also participates in the human condition as God and man. In so doing, Jesus also establishes the Kingdom identified in his preaching.[58] Hartt's explication of this claim provides his answer to the question of the authority and identity of Jesus Christ.

Hartt bases his explication on four broad characterizations of human existence. The first of these is the power of participation:

> Of everything distinctively human it can be said that one participates in it rather than possesses it. Whatever it is, a concrete

---

[56]Ibid., 188. Once again I want to emphasize that Hartt's account does not depend upon an "Ontology" whose truth or persuasiveness can be established independent of his account of Jesus' authority and identity.

[57]Ibid. In this quote and throughout his exposition Hartt obviates the distinction between a Christology from below and one from above.

[58]Ibid., 193.

human person has it under the predicative rather than the substantive mode. I am not Life, I am living.[59]

The second characterization is the distinction between and unity of essence and participative act which is displayed in time by a human life. Rightly understood, the essence of a human life "is its actual and active power of participation."[60] But humanity is continually betrayed into illusion: (1) the belief that essence precedes participation and determines it, thereby eliminating human freedom; (2) the belief that the duality of essence and participation is "that alienation from which all human mischief and misery spring."[61]

The third characterization which Hartt adduces is the human aspiration to overcome the alienation of truth and essence. Hartt describes this overcoming as a condition in which "the act and the object become identical relative to the good of each."[62] This description opens the possibility to a state of perfection in which the subject is not absorbed into the predicate nor the predicate absorbed into the subject. In other words, God and creation may be reconciled with neither losing its identity.[63] But human aspira-

---

[59]Ibid., 188-89. Cf. Hartt's description of historical subjecthood as participation in the storied past and destiny of a community. *TMI*, 189-95.

[60]Ibid., 190. Hartt introduces the notion of history with little fanfare. In chaps. 5 and 6 I will examine his detailed discussion of history which is found in *TMI*, 162-254, and *CC*, 231-91.

[61]Ibid. Here Hartt claims that poets, theologians, and speculative philosophers rightly protest against alienation, but wrongly locate its source and its rectification. This particular critique and affirmation may be read as a response to Kroner, Jaspers, and others. See also Julian N. Hartt, "Human Freedom and Divine Transcendence," *Journal of Religion* 31 (1951): 38-51; idem, "God, Transcendence and Freedom in the Philosophy of Jaspers," *The Review of Metaphysics* 4 (December 1950): 247-58; idem, "On the Possibility of an Existentialist Philosophy," *The Review of Metaphysics* 3 (September 1949): 95-106.

[62]Ibid.

[63]Here Hartt indicates his way of obviating the necessity of deciding at some point for either classical or neoclassical metaphysics. For a critique of Hartshorne's neoclassical metaphysics see Julian Hartt, "The Logic of Perfection," *The Review of Metaphysics* 16 (June 1963): 749-69.

tion to overcome alienation is distorted and misdirected by human creativity apart from the revelation of the Kingdom.

The fourth element of human existence which Hartt identifies is

> a duality of consciousness that reflects the ontological duality of essence and act. Man is at once an actor and a role, as well as an agent and an enterprise. Consciousness doubles back upon the self; and thereby the human being becomes spirit.[64]

If I admit my agency, I must also admit my failure. If I seek to escape this admission by denying my agency, I inflict upon myself a low value which makes the good seem out of reach; or I may deny the duality altogether—which is to renounce my humanity.

In these four characterizations of human existence, Hartt traces the effect of illusion and alienation upon humanity and the descent of humanity into despair and nihilism. The image of humanity as God's creation and redemption has been lost.[65]

Hartt claims that the identity and authority of Jesus Christ are seen in his participation in and command over these elements of human existence. Jesus Christ is the revelation of God and of the real human situation, the real shape of the world. He reveals that our true alienation is from God and that God has reconciled us. In the acceptance of the Kingdom of God in Jesus Christ, the image of humanity as God's creation and redemption can be reborn.[66]

In order to establish his claims, Hartt first argues forcefully that "Jesus Christ is fully human in the expression of his powers of participation."[67] Hartt describes this as "predicational nonidentity," meaning that the world and the actualities of the human situation

---

[64]Ibid., 191.

[65]Along these same lines see *The Lost Image of Man* (Baton Rouge: Louisiana State University Press, 1963), where Hartt traces our culture's loss of images of humanity through contemporary literature.

[66]In this exposition Hartt avoids the language of substance which characterizes classical metaphysics and christology. Nevertheless, Hartt presents Jesus Christ as fully human and fully divine.

[67]Ibid., 193.

are not mere expressions of Jesus' own substance. Participation rather than substance is the way in which to think about Jesus Christ:

> Therefore his Lordship must be seen in his participational power rather than in any antecedent essential identity binding the world into his "substance." "The Father saw fit in his good pleasure to give him all things" is exactly the decisive accent. The supreme expression of participational power in Jesus Christ is his obedience to the Almighty Father.[68]

Hartt further specifies this power of participation as the love which both created and redeems this world. This love finds expression in the futurity of the Kingdom which Christ represents. Jesus Christ's absolute devotion to the Kingdom is not playacting; he does not have "from the beginning of his earthly story what he has at its end."[69] Thus, Jesus Christ participates fully and really in the actualities of human existence.

After introducing Jesus Christ's participation in the human condition, Hartt shows how Jesus displays his command of the elements of the human condition. First, Jesus is victorious over illusion. Jesus knows that his "essence" is directed toward the Kingdom of God and he resists every temptation to betray that essence. Thus, "the father of lies is overcome by the love of Jesus Christ which goes unerringly to its proper object. His participational aim and thrust are perfect, so Satan has no lie at his command for the love of which Jesus Christ can be deflected."[70]

Another element in Jesus Christ's participation in and command of the human condition follows from his victory over illusion: "human aspiration for unity of essence and act is expressed and radically reexpressed in Jesus Christ." Specifically, although Jesus aspires to unity, he directs it not toward overcoming the

---

[68]Ibid. Hartt may seem to have an adoptionist christology at this point. However, he is working in an entirely different field of meaning, with different issues from those which give rise to the accusation of adoptionism.

[69]Ibid., 194.

[70]Ibid., 195.

duality of self and world, but toward overcoming the love of self through "the love of God in the righteousness of the Kingdom." This unity which Jesus Christ expresses both authorizes and energizes the justification, the rectification, the reorientation, of the human condition.[71]

Jesus Christ also participates in the duality of human consciousness. But in his perfect participative unity with the Holy Spirit, duality in him does not become division. He is the same as actor and as agent:

> Jesus is Messiah, and he is Messiah in the depths of his being. His entire being is in his act of participation in God's purpose for man. He is the supreme agent of the Kingdom, agent both in the sense of one who acts, and in the sense of one who represents the interests of another. He holds nothing in reserve for some other role. . . . His life, inner and outer, is in his act. His word is his substance. His essence is in his death on the Cross. He has no role to play, whether it be the role of Messiah, or Sinner, or Prince of the House of David, or King of the Jews, or Prophet, or Priest. He simply is what he proclaims: the righteousness of the Kingdom of God.[72]

Just as Hartt's earlier characterization of the human existence traces the process of alienation and the loss of the image of humanity, his presentation of Jesus' identity traces the process of reconciliation and the rebirth of the image of humanity which is the Kingdom of God.

Hartt expands this claim with an exposition of Jesus' life in the body and in time which shows the duality-in-unity of Jesus' participation in human existence and further delineates the Kingdom revealed in the preaching and person of Jesus Christ. In his exposition Hartt makes a crucial distinction between Jesus' life in the flesh and his life in the body. The flesh, Hartt says, denotes Jesus' participation in the world of matter; the body denotes Jesus' participation in the concrete human world. In his flesh Jesus tired,

---

[71]Ibid., 196.
[72]Ibid., 198.

hungered, slept, suffered; in his body Jesus was perfectly obedient to the Spirit.[73]

Hartt takes Jesus' life in time to be the life of the Lord of time in three ways. First, Jesus perfectly perceives both the time of the Kingdom—it is now—and the time, the timing, of the enemies of the Kingdom. Secondly, Jesus "orders his will to the pace as well as the essence of the Kingdom."[74] Thirdly, Jesus' story is timeless, not in the sense that it cancels or distorts time by the appearance of eternity in time, but in the sense that "what he says of the Kingdom is an embodiment of the Kingdom in his own person [which] brings the powers of God into immediate application upon generic man."[75]

In his participation in and command over the elements of human existence and in his life in the body and in time, Jesus Christ expresses his identity as not just the preacher of the Kingdom but also as the embodiment of the Kingdom. Thus, Hartt shows the unity of the Gospel of the Kingdom of God in the preaching and person of Jesus Christ. To this unity of preaching and person, Hartt adds the "work" of Jesus Christ.

The Work of Jesus Christ. In his chapter on "The Sufficiency of Christ's Work," which he describes as "the thinnest possible sketch of an interpretation," Hartt seeks to show that "the efficacy of the sacrifice of Jesus Christ is the power of the Risen Lord to transform the generic elements of man's being."[76] As he has previously sought to uncover the unity of Christ's preaching and person, Hartt here uncovers the unity of the Cross and the Resurrection—the "work" of Jesus Christ—and at the same time displays

---

[73]Ibid., 198-204. Cf. the less developed discussion of humanity in the context of nature in *TTE*, 43-47.

[74]Ibid., 207.

[75]Ibid., 209. Cf. 142-43, where Hartt criticizes cyclical and linear views of time. In contrast Hartt suggests an affirmation of the periodicity of time, of time's unevenness, in which the Incarnation is the "moment in which the value of the whole process is supremely actual." This, for Hartt, is the meaning of the consummation of time.

[76]Ibid., 229, 211.

the unity of the work with Jesus' preaching and person.[77] Hartt seeks the unity of Cross and Resurrection in Jesus' attack upon the alien powers which hold humanity in unrecognized bondage.[78] Hartt outlines these powers as the spread of the kingdom of sin and death which has seized the ontological fundamentals of humanity's being.

When the kingdom of death seizes *mortality*, it teaches me that something will be going on without me after I die.[79] Thus, either I or "the something going on" is stripped of value, and this future condition gets read back into the present. Ultimately, I seek ways of giving my death value which my life does not have. Thus, death reigns.

Faced with this world which is stripped of value and which strips me of value, I withdraw my *love* and practice "a differential and discriminating hatred: this person and that person, rather than mankind as a whole are the objects of this hatred; but a world magnitude of hatred is concentrated upon them."[80] Alternatively,

---

[77]Hartt may appear to elevate the importance of the Resurrection over the Cross. He says: "If therefore the Christian were confronted with the contrived necessity of choosing between the Crucifixion and the Resurrection, in good faith he would have to choose the latter. . . . Christianly we have to say that the death of Jesus Christ receives its significance from the Resurrection: it is the Resurrection which certifies that he is Lord forever." (CC, 211) But we must also say that the Resurrection receives its significance from the sacrifice of Christ: *this* obedient, loving servant is the one who was raised, who is Lord. Christianly we must say that there is no Christian faith apart from the unity of the crucifixion and resurrection. Hartt's full exposition is consonant with this way of putting the relationship between cross and resurrection, but in my judgement he is unwise to even entertain the contrived necessity of choosing. It opens him to misunderstanding and misrepresentation.

[78]One may be tempted at this point to consider Hartt's account to be a version of *Christus Victor*. While such a characterization is not wrong, it is an oversimplification of Hartt's account, as we will see.

[79]Ibid., 216. Hartt earlier denoted this ontological fundamental as "death." (CC, 70) The change here, I think, is innocuous, probably to avoid the awkwardness of talking about how the kingdom of death corrupts death.

[80]Ibid., 217.

I create a fantasy world which reflects the ego value I seek. In either case I accept the lies of the kingdom of death and serve it.

The possibility of creating a fantasy world shows how the *creativity* of human being is corrupted but not erased by the kingdom of death: "when the heart (the power to love) is in the grip of death, man's creative power is used to curse life and the world."[81]

Human creativity, corrupted by the kingdom of death, also serves to transform *anxiety* into despair. Here human imagination makes the future present and "the line between the present and the future disappears," not metaphysically or commonsensically, but affectively.[82]

Guilt, according to Hartt, is corrupted by the kingdom of death when it is united with time—"a marriage made by man and applauded in hell."[83] Whereas the corruption of anxiety collapses future and present, the corruption of guilt collapses past and present. Now "every project and every prospect seem merely to continue or repeat the past in which he is purely and simply guilty of evil. . . . Judgment is no longer the terror to be anticipated, it is the damnation to be endured forever."[84]

In the light of this spread of the kingdom of death, Hartt displays the unity of the crucifixion and resurrection by showing how Jesus Christ fully participated in both the Kingdom of God

---

[81]Ibid., 218. Hartt draws a provocative distinction between science and poetry as expressions of creativity. Poetry (he singles out Dylan Thomas and Robinson Jeffers) hurls "imprecations against the evils of life in a cosmos from which Providence has vanished." (*CC*, 218) Scientific creativity, on the other hand, is primarily a curse, since it has produced weapons of mass destruction and poisoned creation (*CC*, 218-19). I am not sure Hartt is entirely fair here. Are the various forms of culture and creativity really this distinct? Does not scientific creativity depend, in part, on other expressions of civilization? One of the striking features of Hartt's work is the little attention he gives to "scientific culture," relative to the attention he gives "artistic culture." See Hartt's many reviews of novels, *TTE*, 14-17, and *LIM*.

[82]Ibid., 220.

[83]Ibid.

[84]Ibid., 220-21.

and the kingdom of death. Participating in both kingdoms entailed a unique sacrifice which comprises not only death on the cross but an entire life confronting "every human antidivine propensity."[85] In this confrontation Jesus is sacrifice, but he is never victim. And the efficacy of Jesus' sacrifice stems from the same source as the power of his resurrection: his participation in both kingdoms. Hartt moves then to show how this efficacy of Christ's sacrifice and the power of his resurrection transform the essential elements of human being.

Throughout his exposition Hartt draws out present and future effects of the efficacy of Christ's death and resurrection. We are shown that *death* participates in "the teleology of God's Kingdom."[86] As we participate in that teleology, we must face death. But it has now been "reduced to mortality" and no longer reigns over us.

Love can look forward to the end of all spurious objects of love. Now since death no longer reigns, we can face the world and the enemies' hatred without conforming to it. Love becomes "the first law of being and the source of unalloyed delight."

Creativity hopes for the day when the human spirit will be perfectly at peace with God and creativity will no longer be "unwitting curse or recoil of imprecation." Now, confronted with its true Lord, creativity is "delivered from the spurious necessity of making gods unto itself and out of itself." Since it no longer must sustain the illusion of immortality, creativity may speak a true word to the present age.

Anxiety dissipates with the realization that the Lord of the future is fully present now. Therefore, we can trust the future and "also be content to live wholly unto God in this present moment."

Finally, *guilt* and the past no longer own us. Jesus Christ "does not erase the past," nor does he "stand between me and the guilt my sin earns." Rather, he shows us that neither our past nor our sin can deny his Lordship:

---

[85]Ibid., 224.
[86]All the quotes in this and the following four paragraphs come from *CC*, 226-29.

Whether we live or whether we die, we are the Lord's. Whether we sin or whether we do not sin we are the Lord's. Satan never really owned us. He lied, as always; and for a season—a crazed eternity—we believed him. That season has past. . . . But I can still say No! The difference is that I know now what this negation means: it is a proud salute to nothing.[87]

Summary. In Hartt's re-presentation of the Gospel, he shows its unity in the Kingdom which is revealed in the preaching, person, and work of Jesus Christ. Indeed, he shows that these three cannot be sundered. Together they reveal God and the human situation. But Hartt's exposition of the Gospel is not "a proof of the Christian faith." Rather, it is

a proving, a putting to the test, a demonstration, a showing-forth, an opening-up, an explication, and an elucidation. It will not be a reason for becoming a Christian. It will be the reason why a Christian believes he must preach the Gospel of Jesus Christ as long as he lives and in every way he lives.[88]

Hartt shows why the Christian must "preach the Gospel of Jesus Christ" by showing how in the Gospel of the Kingdom God engages and transforms the elements of human existence so that creation is redeemed. Hartt's exposition is not a proof of the Christian faith, but it is an invitation to believe in God revealed in Jesus Christ and to enter into God's Kingdom. Thus, in his theological critique of culture, Hartt shows how the Gospel makes sense of the world and makes a case for Christian believing. But the nature of the case is not that of a syllogism or mere rationality, it is an invitation to a way of life.[89]

---

[87]Ibid., 229.

[88]Ibid., 164.

[89]See *TMI*, 10, where Hartt concludes that "justification is not so much a matter of being proved right in holding to certain beliefs as it is of being warranted in holding to a course of life."

• Conclusion •

In this chapter we have seen how Hartt re-presents the revelation of the Kingdom in Jesus Christ as the disclosure of God and of the human situation. In this conclusion I will outline the coherence of Hartt's re-presentation with my description of the roles of the Gospel in Hartt's theology. Next I will elaborate on the three aspects of the Kingdom which I introduced earlier in this chapter. Then I will show how all of these elements require and sustain Hartt's conception of theology as cultural critique.

The Role of the Gospel. In the previous chapter I argued that the Gospel serves as revelation, foundation, and authority in Hartt's theology. Now that I have displayed his presentation of the Gospel, I will outline the coherence of my description with his elucidation of the Gospel and show how he, in practice, fulfills his commitments and meets our expectations.

First, the Gospel is the revelation of God and of the shape of the real world. This claim is precisely what Hartt works out in his elucidation of the Gospel. He continually uncovers the illusions by which we misshape our world and shows how Jesus Christ displays the shape of the real world by participating in and redeeming the human situation. But Hartt's claims about the real world disclosed in the Gospel are claims which have no privileged epistemological status. That is, the fact that the Gospel claims that the human situation is thus and so tells us what convictions the Gospel imposes upon Christians, but that the Gospel makes such claims does not in itself justify those claims. As Hartt warns, we must "distinguish confessing that God is the cause of my outlook from making an appeal to divine warrant for the vindication of my convictions and commitments in the eyes of other human beings."[90] Thus, although Hartt claims the Gospel as revelation, that claim does not imprison the Gospel in a private language or world, or in a merely self-referential story or worldview. Rather, Hartt's view of revelation requires him to make sense of "the world in

---

[90]*TMI*, 77.

which we live," in all its lies and illusions, truth and reality, on the basis of the Gospel. This is the aim of a theological critique of culture that is rooted in the Gospel.

Secondly, the Gospel is the foundation of Hartt's theology. Hartt's elucidation of the Gospel coheres with this assertion since he seeks no foundation outside the Gospel. For example, in his elucidation Hartt continually displaces metaphysics as the proper realm of discourse for the first step in theology. In place of metaphysics, he seeks what the Gospel itself presents to us as foundation. What the Gospel presents, says Hartt, is an illumination, transformation, and rectification of human existence. Although Hartt uses various circumlocutions, such as "ontological fundamentals," for our construal of human existence, he does not appeal to them as the foundation for, or validation of, the Gospel. Rather, they are the objects of interpretation, and the Gospel is founded upon and validated by its power to disclose the illusions by which we live, to transform the structures, and to rectify our lives.

Thus, thirdly, the Gospel brings to bear an external, but not an alien, authority. Hartt displays this conviction very powerfully as he describes how Jesus Christ enters into the human condition. The authority which the Gospel brings to bear is the authority of the One who entered fully into the human condition for our salvation. That authority cannot, therefore, be alien. And because it is the authority of Jesus Christ it is not now imposed; it can only be proposed.[91]

In like manner, Hartt's theology and my construal of it can only be proposed; there is no authority by which they can be imposed. Indeed, an attempt to impose them or an appeal to some authority other than their consonance with the Gospel and their success in making sense of the reader's world would falsify the proposal. Thus, all that I can do at any point in my exposition is display Hartt's work as faithfully and clearly as I can, show its coherence and fruitfulness, and its interpretive power. The reader

---

[91]In his concern for the rhetoric of theology and his construal of authority, Hartt anticpates much of the argument in David S. Cunningham, *Faithful Persuasion* (Notre Dame IN: University of Notre Dame Press, 1991).

will find his or her own reasons for accepting or rejecting, in part or in whole, the proposal.

Aspects of the Kingdom. As I noted in my introduction to this chapter, three aspects of the Kingdom revealed in the Gospel of Jesus Christ authorize and demand Hartt's theological critique of culture: the dialectic of the Kingdom, the intelligibility of the Kingdom, and the actuality of the Kingdom. As I noted earlier, these aspects do not exhaust Hartt's presentation of the Gospel nor does Hartt set out to prove that the Kingdom revealed in the Gospel of Jesus Christ has these three aspects. Nevertheless, they are clearly present throughout Hartt's work, and by accentuating them, we can see something of the coherence and complexity of his theology.

The dialectic of the Kingdom holds together creation and redemption. In relation to creation, "the Christian claim is that the power and purpose Jesus Christ reveals in the reconstitution of human existence are precisely the power and purpose by which human existence is originally constituted."[92] In relation to redemption, the Christian claim is that

> the kingdom of God is in the world for reproof, chastisement, and condemnation of the world. But he who judges the world is God, whose ways are not our ways and whose thoughts are not our thoughts. He condemns and chastises for the redemption of the world, because his purpose in all things is a creative one. The pressure of the kingdom of God upon and in the world is one of infinite solicitude. The relentlessness of the kingdom of God is the relentlessness of the divine love, which will not relinquish the world to a condign fate.[93]

This dialectic is present throughout Hartt's interpretation of the Gospel.[94] Jesus preaches the redemption of the Kingdom as "the

---

[92]*CC*, 72.

[93]*TTE*, 69. Cf. *CC*, 97-98, *RQ*, 48-49.

[94]Hartt's use of this dialectic has many implications for human being in history and cosmos which we will explore in chap. 5, and for the theological thinking about metaphysics and history which we will explore in chap. 6.

perfection of the plan of creation."[95] Jesus' identity is expressed in his mastery of the essentials of human existence. That mastery, Hartt asserts, "comes only from the perfection of God's love. This is the power by which all things are created. And this is why Christian faith teaches that God the Almighty Father has done all of His creating through Jesus Christ."[96] And Jesus' work is one with his preaching and person in revealing God's righteousness as the redemption of creation.[97]

This dialectic of creation and redemption reveals the world as inescapably belonging to God; it also reveals the distortions and illusions which threaten and disfigure the created possibility of humanity.[98] In the dialectic of creation and redemption Hartt sees the power of God's love focused upon a lost world. Redemption of God's creation is the purpose of God. The church which faithfully lives by the Gospel of this Kingdom "has no warrant in the Gospel or from the Holy Spirit to reject the contemporary world as though it were a saint trap of Satanic invention." Rather, the Kingdom revealed in Jesus Christ enjoins the church to proclaim the restoration of the plan of creation, the fulfillment of humanity's longings, in the Kingdom given by God. In order to fulfill this calling, the church must discern the illusory, the unreal, the deceptions of the world in the light of the revelation of God in Jesus Christ.[99] Hartt's critique of culture describes just such discipline and discernment for the church.

---

[95]CC, 176.

[96]Ibid., 73.

[97]Ibid., 210.

[98]In Hartt's own theological project, this dialectic of the Kingdom also undergirds Hartt's attention to "ontological fundamentals" and helps us see how that attention does not betray Hartt's theological vision; it is, indeed, an integral part of that vision.

[99]There are many similarities between Hartt and Karl Barth: their preference for "dogmatics," their attitude toward historical criticism, their concern for preaching. However, Hartt's systematic use of the dialectic of creation and redemption clearly distinguishes his work from Barth's. Cf. Hartt's remarks about Barth in Dickerman, *Karl Barth and the Future of Theology*, 43.

The intelligibility of the Kingdom is displayed throughout Hartt's exposition. For example, in Jesus' preaching, the Kingdom is near in its perfect recognizability. In his identity, Jesus is "God's word spoken from within the human condition."[100] Jesus participates fully in human existence; the story of his life takes place in our world—the illusory ones which are human "creations" and the real one which is God's creation. And Hartt's exposition of Jesus' work shows its intelligibility as the transformation of the concrete actualities of human existence.

Although the intelligibility of the Kingdom is rooted in Jesus Christ, it is also the work of the Holy Spirit. In other words, the foundation of the church's vocation is Jesus Christ, but the life of the church is the Holy Spirit.[101] As the Spirit sustains, inspires, and sanctifies the labors of the church, the Spirit also lays upon the church the responsibility intelligibly to proclaim the Gospel:

> [At Pentecost] the Holy Spirit imparted the marvelous power to proclaim the Gospel in whatever tongue was required to make it understood. From this the church correctly concludes that the Gospel is always to be proclaimed in an intelligible tongue. The life of the church thereafter is committed to the translation of the Gospel into the idiom of the contemporary world.[102]

But this demand for intelligibility must not be confused with assimilating the Gospel to the mind of the age or with trimming and fitting the Gospel to meet a culture's criteria for rationality and intelligibility in a quest for relevance. The demand for relevance and intelligibility in the church's proclamation comes not from the culture but from the Gospel. And that demand cannot be separated as a methodological principle distinct from the Gospel; the Gospel is the demand for and the criterion of faithful preaching. Moreover, translating "the Gospel into the idiom of the contemporary world" should not be confused with interpreting the Gospel according to the demands of the present, "trimming" it to

---

[100]*CC*, 192.
[101]*TTE*, chaps. 1, 5, and 6, esp. 61-62; *CC*, 97-98.
[102]*CC*, 133.

fit the mind of the age. Rather, Hartt's concern, as he says elsewhere, is that the theologian "cannot limit his interpretation of the Christian message to biblical language" or to "the language of popular piety."[103]

The church faithfully preaches the Kingdom by exposing the lies and illusions of the world in the light of God's redemption in Jesus Christ. In order to do so, theology must use the idiom of its culture. Hartt's theology of culture serves the fulfillment of that mission by continually examining the cultural situation and the place of the church in the light of the revelation of Jesus Christ.

The actuality of the Kingdom is the third aspect crucial to Hartt's theology. Hartt continually guards the Kingdom against any suggestion of ideality. In the preaching of Jesus Christ, the Kingdom is declared to be present and actual in the human community. The joy and peace given to those who believe in Jesus Christ are not anticipations of the Kingdom, they are participation in the Kingdom now present and actual. In his exposition of the identity of Jesus Christ, Hartt shows how the Kingdom is present but also future, already and not yet. The revelation of the being of humanity in the being of Jesus Christ shows the proper relation of essence and participative act through human participation in the present reality of the Kingdom of God. In his exposition of the cross and resurrection, Hartt shows the actuality of the Kingdom of God in Jesus Christ's triumph over the kingdom of death.

Thus, "what the church preaches is the *actuality of redemption*, which embraces all of mankind and includes the present moment."[104] Hartt does not entomb the Kingdom in the past, in the events of the biblical record. Rather,

> that to which scripture witnesses is a present and wholly concrete actuality, present and concrete in the past, present and concrete now. Therefore, our task is not to conjure this actuality out of the

---

[103]*TMI*, 67. Hartt's subtle and allusive discussion of the language of theology throughout this chapter on "Christian Faith and Conceptual Schemes," is pertinent.

[104]*TTE*, 56, his emphasis.

past but to apprehend its presently real and everlasting character and its real demands upon us.[105]

This present actuality also depends upon the work of the Holy Spirit, for it is the Holy Spirit which makes us "participants in the actualities of redemption."[106] The actuality of the Kingdom here and now underwrites the demand for relevance disciplined by the Gospel in the church's proclamation. If the Kingdom is present and real, then the church is enabled by God the Holy Spirit to proclaim it to the world without assimilating the Kingdom to the world. Again, theology as cultural critique is the enabling of the church's apprehension of the actuality of the Kingdom.

These three aspects of the Kingdom which are displayed throughout Hartt's exposition could also be adduced as corollaries of the role of the Gospel in Hartt's theology. The Gospel of the Kingdom can be the revelation, foundation, and authority for theology in so far as the Kingdom is actual, intelligible, and dialectical. The dependence can also be drawn in the opposite direction: the Kingdom can be shown to be actual, intelligible, and dialectical in so far as the Gospel is the revelation, foundation, and authority for theology. But these elements cannot be separated from Hartt's interpretation of the preaching, person, and work of Jesus Christ. Neither the aspects of the Kingdom nor the roles of the Gospel can be known apart from the Gospel of Jesus Christ. There is a complex and profound interpenetration of these elements in Hartt's theology, but the claims about the roles of the Gospel and the aspects of the Kingdom gain authority and persuasiveness only in Hartt's presentation of the Gospel in the preaching, person, and work of Jesus Christ.

Hartt's Evangelical Theology as Cultural Critique. Now we have the Gospel as revelation, foundation, and authority; the Gospel in the preaching, person, and work of Jesus Christ; and the dialectic,

---

[105]Ibid., 11. To avoid misunderstanding I must note here that for Hartt the church is not the Kingdom. Therefore, "the present and wholly concrete actuality" is not a reference to the church. I develop this distinction in chap. 4.

[106]Ibid., 62.

intelligibility, and actuality of the Kingdom. As I have indicated in my exposition, these elements in Hartt's understanding of the Gospel of Jesus Christ require and support his understanding of theology as cultural critique: "the interpretation of a system of values, creations, and attitudes in the light of and on the basis of the revelation of being and good in Jesus Christ."[107] This task of interpretation also reflects Hartt's description of the aim of theology of culture. According to Hartt, theological critique of culture is to serve the evangelical commission of the church:

> The aim [of theology of culture] is very much more than to discover how far and in what ways a culture falls short of "Christian standards." The aim is to enable the people of the church to discharge more adequately their responsibilities in the present moment. To "save the present age"; that is the aim.[108]

In sum, Hartt's presentation of the Gospel of the Kingdom revealed in Jesus Christ undergirds his theology of culture, displays the creative-redemptive purpose of God, and lays upon the church the vocation to witness to that purpose.

In this chapter we have been examining Hartt's execution of this understanding of theology as cultural critique in light of the Gospel. The christological chapters of *A Christian Critique of American Culture* that have been our concern display in a concentrated and basic way Hartt's presentation of the Gospel as the revelation of God and the human situation, the real shape of the world. By Hartt's own account this work is never complete or final, but it can be faithful to the Gospel, meaningful to the world, and a truthful account of the shape of the real world.

In this chapter I have displayed Hartt's re-presentation of the Gospel as the practice of theology as cultural critique. From beginning to end, Hartt pursues this task in service to the Gospel. In this devotion to the Gospel, Hartt's theology is exemplary of an "evangelical" theology of culture, not by being part of the

---

[107]*RQ*, 49.
[108]*TTE*, 49. Hartt reiterates this in *CC*, 48. See above 7n.15.

Christian subculture of evangelicalism, but by calling us to discern the present reality of the work of Christ revealed and established in the Gospel. Hartt's theology pursues with passion, erudition, and creativity the task of witnessing faithfully to the one who is the good news, who is the Kingdom—Jesus Christ—so that we may apprehend his presently reality and his demands upon us. Since that task is assigned to the church, we must now turn to the place of the church in Hartt's conception of theology as cultural critique.

Chapter 4

The Place of the Church in Hartt's Theology of Culture

> Whenever we reflect upon the life of the church we cannot but marvel at its strangeness—surely it is fearfully and wonderfully made! . . . God calls upon this strange creature to humble itself in "Christian" culture for the glory of His Kingdom. . . . What the church really is, is disclosed in preaching the Gospel in a civilization that contains an immensely varied response to it. To call this civilization Christian is to say that the church cannot escape having to confront and live with the effects of its own life and preaching in history. Such is the judgment of God.[1]

In this chapter, we will investigate the "place" of the church in Julian Hartt's theology of culture. By speaking of the place of the church, I mean to highlight Hartt's concern for the situation of the church, though as we investigate that concern we will also engage questions about the life and the mission of the church.

In the previous chapters I have argued that in Julian Hartt's understanding, the Gospel of Jesus Christ requires the practice of theology as cultural critique, and that such practice serves the vocation of the church to preach the Gospel. Together, these concerns for the practice of theology and for the vocation of the church make ecclesiology one of the central elements of Hartt's theology, along with the Gospel and the world. Indeed, one of the strengths Hartt identifies in theology of culture is that it seeks "to

---

[1]CC, 292.

take the plight of the church with deep seriousness."[2] Therefore, in this chapter we will explore the "place" of the church—not where it is in Hartt's theology, but, rather, where Hartt's theology "places" the church in relation to the Kingdom, the world, and American culture. This approach will not yield a full-blown ecclesiology, but along the way this account will reflect Hartt's concern for the situation, identify the mission of the church, and cohere with Hartt's re-presentation of the Gospel.

• Church and Kingdom •

Since Hartt's theology begins with the Gospel of the Kingdom, one crucial element in his ecclesiology must be an elucidation of the relationship of church and Kingdom which reflects the actuality, intelligibility, and dialectic of the Kingdom. These convictions about the Kingdom of God find expression in Hartt's claim that

> the church is not the Kingdom. The church is the servant of that Kingdom, and it is often timid and often proud. It is persistently weak, corrupt and ambiguous; but withal it is a servant through whose stuttering and fearful whispers and through whose vainglorious clamor the gospel gets itself proclaimed! For which thanks be to God alone.
>
> The church is sent to bear witness to the Kingdom in our midst. It also testifies to the Kingdom that is beyond the world and beyond history. The kingdom of God penetrates and permeates the world; but it stands there over against the world, in invincible holiness. Our world is shattered against it, for the Kingdom is established from everlasting to everlasting, and it will not be moved.[3]

If Hartt were to assert that the church is the Kingdom, then in order to account for the imperfections of the church, he would have to admit that the Kingdom is not actually God and humanity in perfect community. If he were to claim that the church is merely

---

[2]CC, 5. The other strength which Hartt identifies (6) is its quest to attain "the right understanding of the human situation."

[3]TTE, 71; CC, 180.

an anticipation of a future Kingdom, he would be denying the present actuality of the Kingdom. Positively, the church is related to the Kingdom as the church serves and witnesses to the actuality, intelligibility, and dialectic of the Kingdom.

The actuality of the Kingdom carries far-reaching implications for the life of the church. It teaches us that the church and the Kingdom cannot be identified, and that the Kingdom is not a predicate of the church. Kingdom and church are united only as the work of the one Spirit. The Kingdom is the work of the Spirit who incorporates us in the Kingdom. The church has its being through the presence of God as Holy Spirit.[4] The church is not "a thing holy in itself."[5] Rather, to speak of the holiness of the church is to speak about God's actions in the church. Holiness is God's predicate displayed in the church. In so far as the church is faithful to God, God's power is present, making the church holy.[6] In like manner, the Kingdom is not a predicate of the church, but in so far as the church is faithful, the Kingdom may be seen in the church.[7]

Following from this, the assertion that the church is not the Kingdom has great import for the particular difficulties that the empirical reality of the church poses for any theology like Hartt's, with his emphasis on the concrete actuality of the Kingdom and the church's vocation to witness to that Kingdom. What do we do

---

[4]Hartt, *TTE*, chapter 5; *CC*, 292-94. Earlier in *CC* (3-61), Hartt identifies the illusory foundations which tempt the church, particularly in a culture which has been formed in some measure by the church.

[5]*CC*, 293.

[6]When the church is unfaithful it is still the church but it is not holy. See *CC*, 296-97.

[7]Wolfhart Pannenberg takes a similar position in Wolfhart Pannenberg, *Theology and the Kingdom of God* (Philadelphia: Westminster Press, 1969) 76-78: "It is clear that the Church is not to be equated with the Kingdom of God, nor vice versa. . . . Christ points the Church toward the Kingdom of God that is beyond the Church. To the degree that the Church follows his pointing and heeds his reminder, the Kingdom of God will manifest itself through the Church. But note that this is quite different from attributing to the Church in its established structures the dignity of being the Kingdom of Christ."

when the church seems to be the best argument against the actuality of the Kingdom? Hartt describes a typical situation:

> We are called upon to apologize for a great deal in the actual behavior of the church, in fact for so much that theologians are hard pressed to contrive barely plausible rationalizations. In turn the preaching church is called upon to defend these theological speculative rationalizations of the church's real history. These interpretations, compounded of special pleading about history, of loot got from raids on metaphysics, of poetry, and of rhetorical devices concealed as dialectics, have themselves to be defended thereafter as the direct contributions of the Holy Spirit.[8]

This situation, in which the church seems to give lie to its proclamation, can be ameliorated by recognizing that the church is not the Kingdom, that the church is not in itself holy.

If this assertion is kept as a rule then we will not fall into the trap of claiming for the church the predicates of the Kingdom. When the church does cause offense, the issue can be properly framed and answered. At times the church's answer will be confession and repentance, not because the church has failed to be the Kingdom, but because the church has failed to serve and to witness to the Kingdom.[9] In that confession and repentance the church is restored to faithful witness as it points to the God whose Kingdom is judgment and redemption. At other times the answer to accusations against the church will be that the offense is rooted, not in the church or the Kingdom of God, but in that alien kingdom which holds humanity in thrall.

Just as important to Hartt's ecclesiology are two ways the offense of the church will not be answered; both depend upon an implicit identification of church and Kingdom. First, because the Kingdom of God is a present actuality, Hartt cannot say that the church causes offense because it is only potentially the Kingdom,

---

[8]Ibid., 293.

[9]Cf. *CC*, 7, where Hartt says that more serious than the church's irrelevance and attempted self-justification is "our failure to make an honest and steady habit of confessing this sin to God and thereafter to the world."

that is, that it is the Kingdom under construction but not yet complete.[10] To make such a claim Hartt would have to deny the present actuality of the Kingdom and appeal to the Kingdom as a future ideality. Secondly, because the Kingdom is concrete and visible, Hartt cannot have recourse to a distinction between a visible and invisible church which identifies the invisible church with the Kingdom. That identification would deny the concreteness and visibility of the Kingdom.[11]

The corollary of the assertion that the church is not the Kingdom is the assertion that the church is servant of and witness to the Kingdom. Like the former, the latter assertion has its foundation in the actuality of the Kingdom, which is the work of "the Holy Spirit, the continuing presence of the Lord in our midst."[12] Since Pentecost the Holy Spirit has empowered the church's preaching. We have already seen the priority which Hartt assigns to preaching, but our ordinary use of the term to refer to verbal proclamation should not blind us to Hartt's broader use of "preaching" to refer to showing forth, demonstrating, illustrating,

---

[10]This does not deny that the Kingdom has a future aspect. It merely denies that the church can be identified with the Kingdom as already and not yet. Pannenberg (*Theology and the Kingdom of God*, 77) makes the helpful observation that "the main traditional schemes of ecclesiology too readily assumed that the Church (or a particular church) is the present, albeit imperfect, form of the Kingdom of God." (But cf. Wolfhart Pannenberg, *Jesus: God and Man*, 2nd ed., trans. Lewis L. Wilkins and Duane A. Priebe [Philadelphia: Westminster Press, 1977] 373, where he describes the church as a "precursory form of the Kingdom.") The weaknesses in Pannenberg's exposition are (1) his failure to see that Jesus Christ not only proclaimed the Kingdom, but also is the concrete form of the Kingdom, is the Kingdom in his person and work, and (2) his overwrought emphasis on the futurity of the Kingdom. Because of these weaknesses the Kingdom of God plays a diminishing role as Pannenberg's theology develops.

[11]The distinction between visible and invisible church has a complex history. Like all theological issues, it is not one problem. The syntax of the sentence identifies the specific error I want to resist without prejudging every formulation of the visible invisible distinction. However, it is a formula I think we can better do without.

[12]*TTE*, 62.

and exemplifying the Kingdom.[13] The terms "servant" and "witness" better convey the breadth of the Spirit's work in Hartt's understanding.[14]

This broad role of the church as witness to the Kingdom derives from several elements in Hartt's understanding of the Gospel. For Hartt, the Gospel reveals the actuality of the Kingdom in Jesus Christ. But the effect of that revelation takes place within the church, the community in which the Scriptures' "clues" to the human situation "come to effective life" and in which the courage to acknowledge those actualities can be generated and sustained.[15] The actuality of the Kingdom, its embodiment in Jesus Christ, and the interpretation of revelation as truth and command, requires that all of the church's life must be brought under the rule of her vocation to witness to the Kingdom.

So the assertion that the church is not the Kingdom but is witness to the Kingdom, does not license the church to live as she pleases as long as the verbal message is right. The relationship between orthodoxy and orthopraxy is one of mutual implication:

Thus the original Christian education is instruction in the religious life of the Christian community. The religious life is represented as things to be done, to be enacted, and not merely verbally confessed and mentally assented to. The meaning of

---

[13]*CC*, 98.

[14]H. Richard Niebuhr, defines the purpose of the church as *"the increase among men of the love of God and neighbor,"* in H. Richard Niebuhr, in collaboration with Daniel Day Williams and James M. Gustafson, *The Purpose of the Church and Its Ministry* (New York: Harper & Brothers, 1956) 31; his emphasis. Niebuhr's account requires two correctives administered by Hartt's account. First, the confusion of the agency of the church and the agency of the Kingdom should be distinguished. The increase in love is the purpose, the aim, the very presence of God's Kingdom; the church's immediate aim and purpose is to serve and bear witness to that Kingdom. Secondly, the love which is directed toward God and neighbor is not simply proclaimed by Jesus, he does not merely reveal *that* God is love; he also embodies the love of God and neighbor and reveals *what* that love is.

[15]*TTE*, 42.

Jesus Christ is, and not merely entails, the life of obedience in prayer and in loving-kindness.[16]

This understanding of the life of the Christian community looks to the Holy Spirit as the one who graces that common life so that it may participate in the Kingdom of God.

This concern for the life and witness of the church in relation to the Kingdom is also guided by the intelligibility of the Kingdom. Already we have seen the intelligibility of the Kingdom in Hartt's interpretation of the Gospel. The work of the Holy Spirit at Pentecost expresses this intelligibility and commits the church to intelligibility and relevance, not as criteria, but as goals of faithful preaching.[17]

Through his exposition of the intelligibility of the Kingdom, Hartt resists the "theological separation of the nature of the truth committed to the church from content of that truth."[18] Thus, in the Gospel the church has "both a content (a message) and a rhetoric." Hartt separates these two, "abstractly and analytically," in order to attend to the intelligibility of the Gospel.[19]

In the faithful church, says Hartt, the Gospel is accepted

as the disclosure of the actuality and the destiny of man in the Kingdom of God. The original and absolute disclosure is in the life of Jesus Christ. From this disclosure the church receives a language. Thus from the very beginning of the church's life the Gospel is a power of speech.[20]

---

[16]*TCU*, 158. Cf. the notion that belief in God is a construing belief, "a declaration of intention both to 'see' all things as belonging to God and actually so to construe them. Here 'construe' is more than a linguistic-intellectual activity. *It means an intention to relate to all things in ways appropriate to their belonging to God.* (*RQ*, 90; his emphasis) We will examine the notion of construing belief, and James Gustafson's use of it, in chap. 6.

[17]Above, 31-33.

[18]*TCU*, 158. This is one of the points in Hartt's understanding of the interpenetration of method and substance.

[19]*CC*, 324-46.

[20]*CC*, 324.

At this point in Hartt's account, preaching is verbal proclamation, the power of speech, whereby the church "identifies the one for whom it works and under whose authority all things are done by the church in the world."[21] Therefore, the church's preaching of the Gospel seeks to discern and to disclose God's identity in the present actuality of the Kingdom of God. The language which God has given to the church does not point to the preacher or the church, but to Jesus Christ as the disclosure of the Kingdom of God. At the same time as it discloses God's identity, faithful preaching of the Kingdom also discloses the human situation, that in our humanity we are "illusionists, the creators and worshippers of untruth," but also that in God's wisdom and grace God has reconciled us to God's righteousness.[22]

In witnessing to the Kingdom of God, the church's preaching should not be done in the accusative or argumentative mode. Rather, the rhetoric of the Gospel is that of indicative and imperative, of story and command.[23] For Hartt, the church's preaching of the Gospel must be declarative because the Kingdom is an

---

[21]Ibid., 324.

[22]Ibid., 325.

[23]*CC*, 275, 337-44; *TCU*, 140-46. I agree with the thrust of Hartt's argument, although I think the distinctions are a bit overdrawn. Hartt's purpose is to distinguish the first-order language of preaching from the second-order language of theology. In *TCU* (140), he says

> there is much over which to argue in the theological expansion of the gospel. Argument over doctrinal expansion must be clearly distinguished from argument over the root convictions of faith in the revelation of God in Jesus Christ. It pertains to the preaching office of the church to delineate these root convictions as vividly and persuasively as possible, and to insist that one either believes them to be true and binding or one does not. This is the elementary Either-Or of gospel proclamation.

This is the right distinction to make. But even the indicative and imperative proclamation of the Kingdom is a kind of argument. For further discussion of Hartt's concerns see Hartt's "Dialectic, Analysis, and Empirical Generalization in Theology," *Crozer Quarterly* 29 (January 1952): 1-17, and William Wilson's "Spreading the Faith."

actuality. The church cannot faithfully present the Kingdom as a possibility or a suggestion. The Gospel is not the church's ideology. Thus, the "rhetoric of story" indicates that faithful preaching is not the same as moral exhortation or metaphysical speculation. Rather, faithful preaching re-presents Jesus Christ's revelation of God and the human situation in such concrete and local ways that the hearer recognizes himself or herself and by the power of the Spirit becomes a participant in the Kingdom.[24]

The Gospel rhetoric of commandment adds an important element to the church's preaching of the Gospel. Hartt claims that "it is the imperatives that hold the line against the possibility of evaporating the story into an edifying once upon a time. Accordingly, the rhetoric of imperatives is an indispensable part of faithful preaching."[25] Hartt's claim draws out the implication that because the Kingdom is actual, it gives directives for how life is to be lived. In keeping with his analysis of authority and his explication of the dialectic of the Kingdom, Hartt does not see these directives as coercive or as the way to appease God.[26] Rather, the Gospel as commandment is the proclamation that the Kingdom which the Gospel story declares to be actual is not only something to be seen, but also something to be done.[27]

---

[24]CC, 326-27.

[25]Ibid., 338. Hartt picks up on this theme at many points: for example, "Revelation as Truth and Command" (*TMI*, chap. 6, 134-61), "Theological Investments in Story" with responses from Stephen Crites and Stanley Hauerwas, and a reply from Hartt (*JAAR* 52/1: 117-56). Hartt concludes *TMI* with a chapter on "Story as the Art of Historical Truth" (219-54). He ends that chapter by saying that "the New Testament faith is not just a story. It is also a strenuous effort to show how the import of the story must be made out: not only understood but, above all, appropriated" (254). In the next section of this chapter, I will explore thoroughly this concern.

[26]See *TMI*, 145.

[27]Throughout his work Hartt argues, in relation to various themes, the connection between knowing and doing. He argues this in his discussions of the three forms of faith (above, 19-21), of the rhetoric of the Gospel, and of "Revelation as Truth and Command" (*TMI*, 134-61). In the last discussion Hartt argues, among many other things, that God's commandments, in addition to being directives for experience and not merely reports of experience, are also rich in cognitive value.

This rhetoric of imperatives once again directs attention to the whole life of the church in its witnessing to the Kingdom of God. If the church is faithfully to preach and serve the Kingdom of God, then the church's own life must be obedient to the imperatives of the Gospel—but again, not for the purpose of claiming the church as the Kingdom. Rather, the church, through her life witnesses to the intelligibility of the Kingdom of God. The church is enabled in this task by the actuality of the Kingdom of God.

• Church and World •

In order to explore the implications of the dialectic of the Kingdom for the life of the church, we turn to the relationship between the church and the world. Hartt's description of theology of culture, his interpretation of the Gospel, and his account of the vocation of the church anticipate a delineation of this relationship between the church and the world. In the next chapter we will examine the diversity and complexity of Hartt's conception of "world." In this chapter our concern focuses on "world" as the illusions and lies which have corrupted God's creation, and as the object of God's judgment and redemption. In the first chapter we indirectly addressed this issue when we examined Hartt's theology of culture and some of the ways the relationship between Christ and culture has been schematized. In the third chapter we saw more directly how Hartt relates Jesus Christ to the world. In this present discussion I will draw upon those chapters in order to describe Hartt's understanding of the relationship between the church and the world. The primary focus will be on how the dialectic of the Kingdom—creation and redemption—shapes Hartt's description of the relationship between church and world.

In *A Christian Critique of American Culture* Hartt summarizes his understanding of the relationship between the church and the world:

Thus, Christian convictions are not merely statements of policy or disposition.

God demands that His church stand out against the world and yet be prepared to sacrifice itself for real human beings in the real world. The church is under a divine obligation to so preach the Gospel of Christ's Kingdom that the native love of illusion and fear of truth will be understood in their intimate interrelatedness. This interrelatedness is part of the fabric of everyday. This does not mean that the church should despise everyday as inane or demonic. Rather, everyday is to be offered up to the redemption of Jesus Christ.[28]

This description of the church's relationship to the world springs out of Hartt's understanding of the actuality, intelligibility, and dialectic of the Kingdom and the church's vocation as servant of and witness to the Kingdom. As we have seen in the previous section of this chapter, the church's obligation, to offer up everyday to the redemption of Jesus Christ, is carried out in the church's preaching and life.

In his preaching, person, and work Jesus Christ establishes and reveals the Kingdom of creation and redemption. That Kingdom, as an everlasting actuality, discloses the illusions by which we live and the alien Kingdom in which we serve. By disclosing our "worlds" as illusory and alien, the Kingdom of God brings them to judgment, but it is a judgment which redeems. In order to disclose, judge, and redeem the human situation, Jesus Christ entered fully into it and faced every "human antidivine propensity."[29]

If the church is to bear witness of that Kingdom come in Jesus Christ, then the church also must enter fully into the church's "world." Since the Kingdom of God is an everlasting actuality *in the world*, the church cannot separate from the world in order to become the pure Kingdom of God. Thus, confident that Jesus Christ came into a "world" of human creation and yet proclaimed and embodied the Kingdom of God, the church also enters fully into the "world," confident also that the Kingdom which it is given to proclaim triumphs over the principalities and powers that rule

---

[28]CC, 48.
[29]Ibid., 224.

the world.[30] To serve and witness to this Kingdom, the church must also be in the world.

For Hartt, this "worldliness" of the church must be very particular:

> if the church does not have local color, if it does not proclaim and body forth the Word in a response modulated by an acute awareness of the speciality of its immediate environment, the church is an invalid if not a ghost. Really to be the church the congregation must preach the Word to *these* people.[31]

Thus, the church is "against" the world in so far as the world is built on lies and illusions and binds humanity to the kingdom of death. But the church is against the world—and in the world—for the sake of God's creation, for the purpose of exposing the lies and illusions in order that humanity may see the real shape of the world, which is the Kingdom of God.

In order to expose these lies and illusions, the church must practice a certain kind of worldliness. It must be in the world in order to discern the lies and illusions that keep the world from the Kingdom of God. So although it is against the world, the church must be in the world for the sake of its mission, its vocation to the Kingdom of God.

But there are dangers in the church's worldliness. When the church misconstrues its relationship to the Kingdom of God, the church becomes captive to the world of lies and illusions whose overcoming it is to witness. So we must add to the "worldliness" of the church, the "otherworldliness" of the church. Hartt describes this worldliness and otherworldliness as "the rhythm of going out and return."[32]

---

[30]*TMI*, 67-71; In *CC*, 341-42, Hartt draws upon the early church's confrontation with other religions in order to make the same point about the church's current practice. He also notes that being in the world can be more of a problem in a civilization formed in part by the church than in a "pagan" civilization. We will examine his analysis in the next section of this chapter.

[31]*TCU*, 168.

[32]*CC*, 301; see 301-302, 311-20.

For Hartt the church can be faithful to its vocation in the world "only when the church remembers that it has a life apart from the world, a secret life hidden with Christ in God."[33] Although Hartt does not dwell at length on the church's worship, in his ecclesiology the obedience of the church depends upon the practice of worship:

> God calls the church to a secret communion with Himself. The whole of the authentic life of the church in the world derives from the secret life it has in God. This secret communion includes prayer (itself more richly varied than we can pause now to indicate), and celebration of the Lord's Supper. The authority given to the church to preach the Gospel of the Kingdom in Jesus Christ is given in the secrecy of prayer. In the secrecy of the Lord's Supper what was thus given is renewed and confirmed. God is known as the Lord only in the life of prayer. God is known as God the all-loving Father only in the remembrance of the sacrifice of Jesus Christ the Son in the Lord's Supper.[34]

This practice of worship identifies the relationship between church and world as a dialectic. On the one hand, the church's worship is always a secret kept from the world because "the world cannot enter into the depths of God's life without surrendering its own essential and illusory self-sovereignty."[35] On the other hand, the world is present in the church's worship as the world is gathered into God's redeeming love and the church's prayers. Thus, in worship the church learns that her life and mission are rooted in God's own life, but also that her life and mission are for the sake of the world as she witnesses to the Kingdom.

When the church does not renew these convictions in worship, the church begins to misconstrue her relationship to the world. On

---

[33]Ibid., 317.

[34]Ibid., 318. This dependence on worship is missing in *TTE*, but it is present in other works. See *TCU*, 174-76, 179-204; "Some Metaphysical Gleanings from Prayer" (*Journal of Religion* 31, 1951, 254-63.); earlier in *CC* (11-13) Hartt shows how worship corrects an abstractly ontological account of the human situation.

[35]Ibid., 319.

the one hand, if the church begins to think that the secret life she has in God is the sole focus of her mission, she abandons the world to its illusions. On the other hand, if the church begins to think that her mission in the world is the sole focus of her life, she becomes party to the world's illusions. In both cases, the church ceases to be faithful to the actuality, intelligibility, and dialectic of the Kingdom.

When the church has become unfaithful, she recovers her faithfulness in her "secret life." This notion of the secret life of the church bears a resemblance to Bonhoeffer's notion of "secret discipline."[36] For Bonhoeffer it seems that this secret discipline is that which enables the church to identify with the religionless world. However, Kenneth Surin has shown the incoherence and weakness of Bonhoeffer's account and of two attempts to strengthen that account.[37] According to Surin, the problem with Ronald Gregor Smith's positing of a dialectic in Bonhoeffer between the worldliness of God and the "discipline of the secret" is that it entails a contradiction in Bonhoeffer's theology by establishing a lacuna between the religionless world and God's revelation in the believing community. In Hartt's terms, this would entail a betrayal of the actuality of the Kingdom. Ray Anderson's interpretation, that the "discipline of the secret" forms the Christian identity so that the Christian can then be Christ in the world, is fully consonant with Bonhoeffer's theology, but it is not able to meet the challenges of the disenchanted world because it cannot render an immanent critique. In Hartt's terms, this would entail primarily an abandonment of the intelligibility of the Kingdom.

Hartt's account of the secret life of the church meets Surin's objections when it is seen in the context of the rest of Hartt's

---

[36]Dietrich Bonhoeffer, *Letters and Papers from Prison*, enl. ed., trans. Eberhard Bethge (London: SCM Press, 1971), 280-81.

[37]Kenneth Surin exposes Bonhoeffer's notion to a searching analysis in "*Contemptus Mundi* and the Disenchantment of the World: Bonhoeffer's 'Discipline of the Secret' and Adorno's 'Strategy of Hibernation,'" in Kenneth Surin, *Turnings of Darkness and Light: Essays in Philosophical and Systematic Theology* (Cambridge: Cambridge University Press, 1989) 180-200.

theology. To the dialectic of creation and redemption Hartt adds the notion of "world" as a human creation full of illusions, lies and deceptions mixed in with truth and reality. The beat of the rhythm of the church's life which carries it into the secret life is rooted in the dialectic of the Kingdom; this beat disciplines the church to see and judge rightly the illusions of the world by the revelation of the Kingdom. The beat of the rhythm of the church's life which carries it out into the world is rooted in the recognition that the vocation of the church is to re-present in its whole life the Kingdom which has overcome the world of lies and illusions. In the secret life of prayer and Eucharist the church surrenders her illusions, she dies to the world; and she is raised into the truth of the world, the newness of the Kingdom.[38] Thus, by drawing on (1) his understanding of "world" as a human creation which is a mixture of illusion and deception, truth and reality, and (2) his understanding of the Gospel as the exposure of the illusions and the revelation of the truth, Hartt places the secret life of the church within the context of overcoming the "world" (of illusion) for the salvation of the world through the actuality of the Kingdom.

In so doing, Hartt provides a coherent account of the church's life in the world as servant and witness of the Kingdom. Hartt's "worldliness of the church" is not identity with the world but identity with the Kingdom which is actually present in the world to redeem the world. Thus, Hartt's "worldliness of the church" enables, in Surin's terms, an immanent critique of the disenchanted world.[39] The secret life of the church, on the other hand, enables a

---

[38]*CC*, 319. See Ray Anderson, *Historical Transcendence and the Reality of God* (Grand Rapids: Eerdmans, 1975) 227-51, for a difficult and provocative treatment of this issue along similar lines.

[39]Hartt wrestles with the problem of secularity at several points. See in particular his attempt to show "that the sense a Christian can discover in secularity is superior to the account a secularist provides of the same phenomenon" (*RQ*, 97-113). Hartt argues that "secularity at its best is an eloquent plea for the commonwealth of man. As such it is a powerful rebuke to Christians living in bad faith. But the proper response to such a rebuke is not to abandon the Christian faith. It would be better to practice it" (113).

transcendent critique of the world that exposes the ways in which the world is not the Kingdom.

• Church and American Culture •

Hartt's exposition of the actuality, intelligibility, and dialectic of the Kingdom, requires him to attend to particular cultures. Likewise, his understanding of the relationship between church and Kingdom, and church and world, means theology must attend to the relationship between the life of the church and particular cultures. This leads to the importance of a third relationship in Hartt's thought: the relationship between church and American culture. A delineation of this relationship is required by Hartt's understanding of the Kingdom as the disclosure of the actualities of the human situation and by his understanding of "world" as an illusory misconstrual of the human situation.[40] If the church in "America" is to serve and witness to the Kingdom in its culture, then its relationship to that culture must be a practical concern of ecclesiology. The church can be faithful to its vocation only if it understands the threats to its faithfulness in the culture and the illusions which bind people in that culture to an alien kingdom.

In the following chapter we will examine Hartt's representation and critique of American culture. In this section we will examine Hartt's judgment of the relationship of the church to American culture under two aspects: (1) the threats posed to the church by American culture; (2) the possibility of communicating the Gospel in American culture.

The threats posed to the church by American culture are those which a "Christian civilization" poses. By "Christian civilization" Hartt means that "the church cannot escape having to confront and live with the effects of its own life and preaching in history."[41] In America the church has been preaching for so long that there are peculiar threats posed to its faithfulness. The popularity and

---

[40]Here I anticipate to some extent the next chapter. See *CC*, 13-48; *RQ*, 97-113.
[41]*CC*, 292.

success of the church can become "a terrible failure"[42] when the church's success dulls its critical edge so that it sees its vocation to preach the Gospel as superfluous in culture that has "already heard." Moreover, "success" may lead the church to think that its being is founded in the world and its mission is expressed in the idealities of culture.

At this point, the church misconstrues the Gospel and the Kingdom. The Kingdom of God becomes the kingdoms of this world and of their christs. The church then becomes irrelevant to the real needs of the culture or seeks its justification not in the Gospel, but in its own life in the world.[43]

Hartt meets these threats by showing that the notion of "Christian civilization" misconstrues the relationship of Kingdom, church, and world. Hartt identifies several different conceptions of "Christian civilization," but all have one thing in common: they seek to assimilate the life and mission of the church to the aspirations of culture in a way that denies the Kingdom of God revealed in Jesus Christ. In this attempted assimilation of the church, Christian civilization often offers the church a place of honor: as the purveyor of the piety of civilization, as the guardian of morals, as the source of creativity.[44] When the church accepts one or more of these offers "the church is taken for granted as a feature and component of everyday, of the present world, rather than as the ordained herald of another world. As a component of everyday the church acts as the guardian of the ideals of civilization."[45] Once the church is assimilated to the everyday of Christian civilization, its fate is bound to that of everyday. And when everyday begins to suffer so does the "faith" of the church.[46]

But all of the offers made by "Christian civilization" are spurious representations of the purpose of the church: "the church was not planted in the world to govern it as a regal presence clearly

---

[42]Ibid., 4.
[43]See Hartt's delineation of these two threats in CC, 41-48.
[44]Ibid., 43-47, 49-61, 302-11.
[45]Ibid., 42.
[46]Ibid., 46.

born to rule. It is here to preach the Kingdom of God."[47] When the church forgets her calling to witness and serve this Kingdom, and instead witnesses and serves "civilization," she has failed. If the church recognizes this failure, she faces two temptations. One is to perpetuate the error by seeking to gain control of civilization, often through civil piety, morality, or creativity. The other is to abandon the world as fallen and beyond redemption. The church recovers from her failure and overcomes these temptations through the rhythm of her life of going out into the world and coming in to her secret life with God, which restores the church to health and enables her "to endure existence in tension with contemporary civilization, looking upon the world neither as an enemy ripe for destruction nor as its patron and keeper."[48]

The rhythm of the church's life makes possible the communication of the Gospel in a way that represents to contemporary hearers the human situation as revealed in Jesus Christ. In so doing, the church claims its proper place in relation to the world. In order to do this

> Christian reflection has to endure the pain and confusion of a categorial revolution, or prove faithless to the Holy Interpreter by using the old categories in the old way. God requires the church to communicate the Gospel rather than to mutter to itself. Thus the church must use a language already in existence; but it must conform this language to the world revealed in Jesus Christ rather than to the old world.[49]

This account of language, as it undergirds the church's faithful proclamation, depends upon the Gospel of the Kingdom which is actual and intelligible. If the Kingdom is not actual, then the

---

[47]Ibid., 310.

[48]Ibid., 311. This concern is evident at the very beginning of Hartt's work; see *TTE*, 9-10.

[49]Ibid., 231-32. In his talk about "language" and "worlds" Hartt anticipates the current debate over intratextual and extratextual approaches to theology. However, Hartt's emphasis on the Kingdom shifts the focus away from "textuality" and onto vision. And his claim that the Gospel reveals God and the human situation combines emphases from both approaches.

church is communicating its own power of language. If the Kingdom is not intelligible, then the church has nothing it can communicate. Thus, to be faithful to its evangelical commission the church must maintain the rhythm of its coming in to its secret life, where it learns the shape of the real world revealed in Jesus Christ, and its going out, where its communicates that revelation, that Kingdom, to the world of lies and illusions.

The church's language and stance in proclaiming the Kingdom to the world of "Christian civilization" is prophetic. Prophecy in this context is "diagnostic rather than predictive."[50] It reveals the human situation before God and lays upon its time the particular demands of God. Efficacious prophecy draws upon the story of the Kingdom in order to throw its hearers "upon corporate memory, in penitence and in gratitude."[51] This prophetic calling of the church is amplified in distinctions Hartt draws between prophet and heretic, and between prophet and prophetic voice.

Hartt's distinction between prophet and heretic implicitly draws on his understanding of the dialectic of the Kingdom.[52] Both the heretic and the prophet proclaim judgment upon an existing order, but on different bases. The heretic seeks to displace the absolute presuppositions of a civilization in favor of his own: "it is in fact his intention to bring the existing order down in ruins and to substitute another one." The prophet, on the other hand, seeks to call the order into judgment before the absolute presuppositions which are "verbally" and "formally" accepted but concretely abrogated. Thus, the prophet does not look to new presuppositions—that would be idolatry—nor does she advocate reversion to the past. Rather, the prophet's "theme is repentance—the fresh grasp upon the absolute presuppositions of human existence, upon the necessities in the grain of being—repentance and then the laying

---

[50]Ibid., 316.

[51]Ibid., 315.

[52]Hartt develops this distinction in answer to R. G. Collingwood: "Metaphysics, History, and Civilization: Collingwood's Account of Their Interrelationships," *Journal of Religion* 33 (1953): 198-211. This may also be read as a response to Emil Brunner's theology of culture. See above.

hold of the contemporary crisis by wills thus clarified and empowered."[53]

Although Hartt does not avow it here, he is drawing on his understanding of the dialectic of creation and redemption in order to establish a place for the church to render a critique of civilization. The Kingdom reveals the real shape of the world: human existence is founded upon God's creation and redemption. No matter how we struggle against it, our only source of existence is the God revealed in the Gospel of Jesus Christ. So, in her critique, the church does not call civilization to some other foundation, as would the heretic. Rather, the church calls civilization to its one true foundation. Therefore, as prophet, the church calls humanity to repentance, to a fresh grasp of God and humanity as revealed in Jesus Christ.[54]

So far Hartt's description of the church as prophet establishes the church as critic of all civilizations, not just "Christian civilization." Hartt responds to the church's situation in the "Christian civilization" which is American culture in his distinction between prophet and prophetic voice.[55]

Hartt sees the church as the present-day successor to the prophet, but he draws a careful distinction between "the prophet"

---

[53]Ibid., 204.

[54]Cf. the instructive distinctions Cornel West makes among "*critique*: the demystifying of an apparent static surface and the disclosing of an underlying process whose emergence negates, preserves, and transforms this surface. . . . *criticism*: the "civil" procedure of endless correction while remaining on the surface. . . . *deconstruction*: a potentially radical yet ultimately barren operation of ingeniously dismantling humanist thought and (attempting to) disarm dialectical reflection." Cornel West, "On George Lukacs," in *Keeping Faith: Philosophy and Race in America* (New York: Routledge, 1993) 143. In these terms, Hartt clearly intends a critique of culture.

[55]*RQ*, 42-49. I will take "propheticism" in this passage to be the same as "prophetic voice." Hartt is not clear on this, but it is clear that the church as prophet is contrasted both to the "prophetic voice" and to "propheticism." As usual Hartt does not specify who he has in mind in this critique of the "prophetic voice." One candidate I would suggest is Reinhold Niebuhr, but I see nothing to be gained in this context from an extended argument in support of Niebuhr's candidacy.

and "the prophetic voice." The prophetic voice draws "inferences concerning the social order from a presupposed philosophical-theological discipline" and consequently is vulnerable to accusations of special pleading and cultural relativism. In contrast, the church as prophet, proceeds with its cultural critique from "its intuitions of the ground of human existence and of the world" as revealed in Jesus Christ. In this critique the church points not to a past or once-upon-a-time Kingdom, but to the Kingdom as a present actuality: "the church's ultimate critique of culture is not derived from any theoretical structure, not even (especially not!) from its own systematic or dogmatic doctrines. Its critique is grounded in and expresses the *living* word."[56] Here once again the actuality of the Kingdom undergirds and guides Hartt's assertions.

Theology of culture, for Hartt, "is one expression of the church's vocation as prophet."[57] Unfortunately, in pursuing this vocation the church is often ensnared by ideology. In order for the church to offer a prophetic critique of culture, theology of culture must attend to ideological snares and to the ultimate questions and theoretic structures which concern philosophy of culture in order to free the church and enable the church's proclamation of the Kingdom as actual and intelligible.

In addition to these distinctions between heretic and prophet, prophetic voice and prophet, the influence of the actuality of the Kingdom can be seen in Hartt's differentiation of theology of culture from "propheticism." First, whereas for propheticism God's judgment is present but God's Kingdom is future, for the Christian theologian the "kingdom has been revealed both to and in history." In this revelation, God demands love, not merely justice. Secondly, whereas for propheticism the power for renewal and repentance resides in the human spirit and the people of God, for Christian faith and theology of culture "power for regeneration and transformation of culture comes in from beyond. This is the

---

[56]Ibid., 43-44.
[57]Ibid., 46.

power of the kingdom now in history; but even though the kingdom is in history, it is still from God and of God."[58]

This prophetic calling requires the church forever to be a critic of its own life and of culture. Because it is not the Kingdom, the church, as we have already seen, "inevitably illustrates the judgment of God's righteousness in its own life."[59] But because it has a secret life rooted in the Kingdom, the church does have a place to stand as critic of culture. In this critique, however, the church must continually point, not to an ideal representation of a civilization's aspirations, but to the Kingdom of God which is the redemption of the aspirations of God's creation made everlastingly actual in Jesus Christ.

• Conclusion •

In this chapter I have sought to display Hartt's ecclesiology in relation to his interpretation of the Gospel, particularly in relation to the actuality, intelligibility, and dialectic of the Kingdom. My purpose has not been to present a fully developed ecclesiology. Rather, I have sought to analyze Hartt's understanding of the place of the church in relation to the Kingdom, the world, and American culture and at the same time address some issues regarding the church's life and mission.

My exposition has inevitably flattened out some of the complexity of Hartt's ecclesiology. In this conclusion I will try to restore some of that complexity by considering Hartt's placing of the church in relation to two current debates.

One lively area of debate concerns the "sectarian" character of the church. A formidable element in that debate is H. Richard Niebuhr's well-known and influential *Christ and Culture*, in which Niebuhr posits five types of answers to the question of the relationship between Christ and culture.[60] Hartt's ecclesiology contains

---

[58]Ibid., 47.

[59]CC, 314.

[60]H. Richard Niebuhr, *Christ and Culture* (New York: Harper & Row, 1951). Although I think there are deep weaknesses and dangers in Niebuhr's typology,

elements of each of Niebuhr's types except "Christ and Culture in Paradox." Jesus Christ is "against" culture in so far as culture is a "world" built on lies and illusions, binding humanity to the kingdom of death.[61] Jesus Christ is "of" culture as the ground of human existence, as the One through whom God does all God's creating. Jesus Christ is "above" culture as culture is put to work in witnessing to the illusions of the world and the reality of the Kingdom of God. Jesus Christ the "transformer" of culture is perhaps the most accurate description to apply to Hartt, but only if the position is opened up to include elements of the other positions.

Hartt's ecclesiology is as complex as this brief summary of his view of the relationships between Christ and culture. The church is against the world for the sake of God's creation, for the purpose of exposing the lies and illusions in order that humanity may see the real shape of the world, which is the Kingdom of God. In order to expose these lies and illusions, the church must practice a certain kind of worldliness. So although it is against the world, the church must be "of" the world for the sake of its mission, its vocation to the Kingdom of God.

Thus, Hartt's ecclesiology is a complex, flexible blend of sectarian and nonsectarian views. The most important element in

---

its popularity makes it an important point of reference. One of the problems with Niebuhr's book is that it implies that certain ecclesiologies follow from certain ways of relating Christ and culture. But the implications are not as clear as Niebuhr suggests and ecclesiologies are in reality more complex than Niebuhr's types. I intend an implicit criticism of Niebuhr in showing that Hartt includes elements from four of Niebuhr's types. For direct criticism of Niebuhr, see John Howard Yoder, Diane M. Yeager, and Glen H. Stassen, *Authentic Transformation: A New Vision of Christ and Culture* (Nashville: Abingdon Press, 1996), and Michael Scriven, *The Transformation of Culture* (Scottdale PA: Herald Press, 1987). Yoder makes the important point that Niebuhr has a monolithic view of culture which disallows a polyvalent judgment of culture, and Scriven shows that a "sectarian" ecclesiology does not necessarily entail a rejection of the world or a denial of the church's mission in the world.

[61]For Hartt "world" is not a monolithic evil. In the previous two chapters we have noted his appreciation for artistic contributions to our understanding of the human situation. In the next chapter we will look more closely at Hartt's polyvalent use of the concept "world."

this complex ecclesiology is the priority assigned to the Kingdom/world distinction over the church/world distinction. In other words, the Gospel is about the Kingdom before it is about the church. But the Kingdom revealed in the Gospel is also about the world. Furthermore, the Gospel is also about the church, that is, the Gospel intends the church.

By maintaining the Kingdom/world and church/world distinctions in their proper order, Hartt provides an ecclesiology which is and is not sectarian. Hartt's ecclesiology is sectarian in the way it construes the Kingdom and the relationship of the church to the Kingdom and the world such that it rejects any Constantinian role for the church. Hartt's ecclesiology is also sectarian in its demand for a communal life which generates and sustains witness to the Kingdom of God in Jesus Christ. Hartt's ecclesiology is not sectarian in the way it construes the Kingdom and the relationship of the church to the Kingdom and the world such that it rejects the withdrawal of the church from the world. It is also not sectarian, because Hartt's interpretation of the Kingdom disallows the rejection or denial of the world. In this balance Hartt's ecclesiology corresponds to his interpretation of the Gospel of the Kingdom as dialectical, intelligible, and actual.

In the end, Hartt's differentiation of Kingdom, church, and world, exposes the flaw in the debates over the sectarian character of the church. These debates are confused because they depend upon the exclusion of the Kingdom of God and a concentration on the church-world relationship. Only in this misconstrual does debate about sectarianism have any power. When the Kingdom is added to the mix, the charge of sectarianism loses its force and the rhythm of the church's life and her place in the Kingdom and the world is properly identified.

If the church is to maintain the rhythm of her life and her place, then the life of the church requires considerable attention. Although Hartt clearly affirms the importance of the whole life of the church for effecting, sustaining, and embodying the witness to the Kingdom of God, he does not attend in any detail to the concrete life of the church as a community which generates a prophetic critique of a culture and an illuminating proclamation of the

Kingdom and its demands.[62] He provides the rationale for the church as that community and even points to the foundation of such communal life in preaching and the sacraments.[63] But he does not delineate the characteristics of such a community with the same depth and insight displayed in his analysis of American culture.

This lacuna in Hartt's ecclesiology is filled in the work of Stanley Hauerwas, who has been influenced at many points by Hartt.[64] Hauerwas's work attends insightfully at many points to the kind of concrete life the church must practice in order to carry out its mission.[65] He develops an ecclesiology, rooted in the Gospel narrative, which attends to the virtues and practices requisite for the sustenance of a community which witnesses to the Kingdom of God. Thus, Hauerwas recognizes and shows more clearly than Hartt the connection between the church's vocation to witness to the Kingdom and the kind of community the church must be in order to generate and sustain the perception of and witness to the Kingdom.[66]

However, there is a danger in giving so much attention to the church: it seems at times to make the church rather than the Kingdom the first priority of theology. Thus Hauerwas's critics attack the way he draws the distinction between the church and the

---

[62]John Howard Yoder offers the same criticism of Hartt in *The Priestly Kingdom*, 202n.11.

[63]See above, 97-100.

[64]Jonathan R. Wilson, "From Theology of Culture to Theological Ethics: The Hartt-Hauerwas Connection," *Journal of Religious Ethics* 23/1 (Spring 1995): 149-64.

[65]See Stanley Hauerwas, *A Community of Character: Toward a Constructive Christian Social Ethic* (Notre Dame IN: University of Notre Dame Press, 1981); idem, *The Peaceable Kingdom: A Primer in Christian Ethics* (Notre Dame IN: University of Notre Dame Press, 1983); idem, "The Church as God's New Language," in Garrett Green, ed., *Scriptural Authority and Narrative Interpretation* (Philadelphia: Fortress Press, 1987) 179-98.

[66]Although it is not couched in terms of witness to the Kingdom, the work of L. Gregory Jones, *Transformed Judgment: Toward a Trinitarian Account of the Moral Life* (Notre Dame IN: University of Notre Dame Press, 1990), attends to these same issues in very helpful ways.

world. But that is not the most basic conflict. The most basic conflict is over the Kingdom/world distinction.[67] Once that distinction is drawn in a manner like Hartt's, then something like Hartt's ecclesiology or Hauerwas's more developed account ineluctably follows. So although Hauerwas's critics, and at times perhaps Hauerwas himself, construe his work in a way inimical to Hartt's ecclesiology, I think that it is rooted in the same distinctions that Hartt makes and contributes significantly to an account of the church which can sustain its vocation to the evangelical commission to witness to the Kingdom come in Jesus Christ.

Finally, the complexity of Hartt's ecclesiology may also be displayed in relation to Avery Dulles's *Models of the Church*—as institution, mystical communion, sacrament, herald, and servant.[68] For Hartt, acknowledging the church as an institution acknowledges an undeniable reality about the place of the church in relation to the world. But it also arms the church against self-delusion by empowering criticism of the church's institutional life.[69] Hartt represents the church as mystical communion in his assertion that the life of the church is the Holy Spirit, but Hartt does not identify

---

[67]At this point there seems to be a tension, perhaps an indecision, in Hauerwas's work. At times he affirms the priority of the Kingdom: "To be sure, God's kingdom is more determinative than the church. . . . " ("The Church as God's New Language," 194); "This kingdom sets the standard for the life of the church, but the life of the kingdom is broader than even that of the church. For the church does not possess Christ; his presence is not confined to the church. Rather it is in the church that we learn to recognize Christ's presence outside the church" (*The Peaceable Kingdom*, 97). But at other times the attention he devotes to the church threatens to overwhelm the priority of the Kingdom. In particular his description of the church as "the foretaste of the kingdom" and his claim that "the church is a social ethic" (ibid., 97, 99) seem at odds with Hartt's position and in tension with Hauerwas's other statements. To describe the church as "foretaste of the kingdom" tends toward denying the present actuality of the kingdom; to claim "the church is a social ethic" tends toward identifying the church and the kingdom. Hauerwas clearly does not intend either of these conclusions, but the claims need clarification.

[68]Avery Dulles, *Models of the Church*, exp. ed. (Garden City NY: Image Books [Doubleday], 1987).

[69]CC, 296-300; TCU, 164-67.

the church with the Kingdom.[70] In witnessing to the Kingdom in the whole of her life, the church is sacramental. But "even if we were to say that the church alone administers salvation, we ought not to suppose that this salvation is its personal property. There is saving grace. There is no saving church."[71] In contrast to Dulles's model of the church as servant, which views the church as servant of the world, Hartt sees the church as servant of the Kingdom. Yet when one adds the dialectic of the Kingdom to this conception, the church becomes the servant of the world in obedience to the creative-redemptive Kingdom.

Finally, Hartt's ecclesiology most resembles Dulles's model of the church as herald. For Hartt, the evangelical commission of the church is primary. The church proclaims the Gospel of the Kingdom revealed in Jesus Christ. But Hartt does not impose the strict distinction between the church's temporal reality and the Kingdom's eschatological (future) reality which Dulles identifies in other representatives of this model.[72] To be sure, for Hartt the church is not the Kingdom, but witness to the Kingdom. Nevertheless, the Kingdom is present and actual here and now. Hartt also resists the existentialist version of this model by affirming the institutional aspect of the church and reversing the movement of dependence in the "language-event" of preaching. Preaching depends upon the presence of the Kingdom, not vice versa.[73] Finally, Hartt's broadening of "witness" to include all of the church's life answers Dulles's criticism that this model neglects "the incarnational aspect of the Christian revelation," the continuity of the Christian community in history, and the call to action.[74]

---

[70]*TTE*, 60-66; *CC*, 299: "The church comes to be by the word, the given pledge, of God, not by the consent of the members."

[71]*TCU*, 164.

[72]Dulles, *Models of the Church*, 79, cites the view of Hans Kung.

[73]The representative theologians here are Bultmann, Fuchs, and Ebeling. See Dulles, *Models of the Church*, 80-82.

[74]Ibid., 84-88. Dulles commends an additional model in a chapter added to the original edition of *Models of the Church* under the heading "The Church: Community of Disciples" (204-26). Dulles does not suggest that this model supplants the others, but he does think it particularly appropriate to the cultural situation of the

In this chapter we have examined how Hartt's theology "places" the church in relation to the Kingdom and the world. These relationships make the life and mission of the church immeasurably complex. As the church seeks to live out her life as servant of and witness to the Kingdom, she is called also to stand as prophet in the midst of a world of lies and illusions. In order to fulfill this calling, the church's theology must engage in a prophetic theology of cultural critique. Such prophetic theology will call the world to discern and to participate in the present actuality of the Kingdom of God. In its dialectic of creation and redemption, this Kingdom makes possible our very existence and grounds all of our human effort to "create" a world. As our "creative" efforts are distorted by sin, this Kingdom judges the world—in order to redeem the world. Rooted in actuality and in the dialectic of creation and redemption, this Kingdom becomes intelligible to the world in the work of the church as prophet, enabled by the Spirit to render a theological critique of culture. Hartt's own re-presentation of the Gospel of the Kingdom gives warrant for believing that this commission to the church and to theology is enabled by the Spirit—and for so acting.

---

church in North America. In this concern for the situation and even the account he gives, Dulles closely resembles Hartt. (See esp. the "rhythm" of the church's life compared to the diastolic and systolic rhythm of the heart, 220-22; cf. CC, 300). However, Dulles stills lays less emphasis than Hartt on the church as herald. Hartt's ecclesiology sees the discipline of the church as servant of the church's mission. Thus, he continually thrusts the life of the church out into the world—in service to the Kingdom.

Chapter 5

The Critique of World in Hartt's Theology of Culture

> The kingdom of God is in the world for the reproof, chastisement, and condemnation of the world. But he who judges the world is God, whose ways are not our ways and whose thoughts are not our thoughts. He condemns and chastises for the redemption of the world, because his purposes in all things is a creative one. The pressure of the kingdom of God upon and in the world is the pressure of infinite solicitude. The relentlessness of the kingdom of God is the relentlessness of the divine love, which will not relinquish the world to a condign fate.[1]

Hartt's conception of "world" has been implicitly present in his conception of theology as cultural critique, his re-presentation of the Gospel, and his ecclesiology. In Hartt's theology, culture is not something that we attend to at the end of the theological task; rather, the question of culture pervades our theological work from beginning to end. Thus, Hartt's re-presentation of the Gospel also contains within it an interpretation of our culture. Likewise, Hartt's discussion of the church concerns, in large part, the relationship between the church and cultures.

In these treatments of culture we already have a preliminary sketch of Hartt's understanding of "world." In relation to theology as cultural critique, "world" is the system of values, creations, and attitudes that is interpreted "in the light of and on the basis of the

---

[1]*TTE*, 69.

revelation of being and good in Jesus Christ."[2] In relation to the Gospel, "world" is that which is God's creation and redemption. In relation to the church, "world" is the threat to and possibility for the fulfillment of the church's mission. These three relationships will be woven into this chapter as we focus on Hartt's conception of "world."

In his critique of culture, Hartt anticipates many recent intellectual developments, such as culture studies and critical social theory. Many of his analyses, written in the 1960s and 1970s seem prescient or, in his terms, prophetic. His analyses provide a basis and direction for an illuminating critique of our present circumstances. My primary purpose here, however, is not to present such a critique; rather, my purpose here is to make Hartt's analyses and insights available so that others may pursue that task.[3] At the end of our examination of Hartt's critique of culture, I will suggest some ways in which his critique may direct our present task.

"World" is a complex concept in Hartt's theology, just as it is in the New Testament.[4] For example, world can be used to refer to everything God has created; or it can be used to refer to everything which is not approved by God, or that which does not know God; or it can be used to refer to that which God loves and Jesus Christ has saved. All of these play some role in Hartt's theology.

We will develop our understanding by beginning with Hartt's description of "world" as human culture and civilization. After examining this somewhat formal account of world as civilization, we will then see how the Gospel of the Kingdom shapes Hartt's analysis. Finally, we will examine some aspects of his interpreta-

---

[2]*RQ*, 49.

[3]I pursue such a critique of our present circumstances in two other books, *Living Faithfully in a Fragmented World: Four Lessons for the Church from MacIntyre's "After Virtue"* (Valley Forge PA: Trinity Press International, 1996) and *Gospel Virtues: Practicing Faith, Hope, and Love in Uncertain Times* (Downers Grove IL: InterVarsity Press, 1997), and in two essays in progress, "Discerning the Demonic: Violence and a Redemptive Ontology of Peace," and "Daring to Die: Giving Up Christian Civilization."

[4]For the reader's sake I will drop the scare quotes around the term "world," though the reader should continue to supply them throughout the chapter.

tion of culture. In this approach, we will once again have in view the coinherence of Gospel, church, and world in Hartt's thought.

• "World" and Civilization •

The "world" which Hartt keeps in view throughout his work is a human achievement. In his early book, *Toward a Theology of Evangelism*, Hartt says that the "world" to which the church proclaims the Gospel is "civilization and culture rather than the whole of the created order, or the order of history and of time."[5] What Hartt means by this description and why it is most significant for his work becomes apparent as he develops a "natural history" of a civilization and examines civilization in the light of the Gospel.

Throughout his work, Hartt refers to culture, civilization, world, the present age, the mind of the age. He does not always make careful, discrete use of these terms. At times he seems to use them more impressionistically than analytically; this does not diminish their power. Indeed, as Hartt moves these words away from conceptual analysis and into imaginative, homiletical rhetoric, they become more vivid and persuasive. Nevertheless, our first concern will be his analytic of culture, civilization, and world.[6]

For Hartt, civilization is an achievement of human creativity confronted by nature and history.[7] In *A Christian Critique of American Culture* Hartt develops this signification of world. There Hartt's description of the relationships between culture, civilization and world, and his conception of "everyday world," are not required by the Gospel.[8] However, the analysis does display his understanding of "world" as a human creation and prepares the way for understanding his construal of the world in relation to the Kingdom.

---

[5]*TTE*, 68.

[6]*CC*, 15-18.

[7]The coinherence of Hartt's theology is evident in the fact that some aspects of this "world" of human civilization were identified and criticized earlier in Hartt's interpretation of the Gospel.

[8]See his similar claim in *TTE*, 69. The discussion in *CC*, 3-61, is an expansion of the earlier analysis in *TTE*, 68-69.

Hartt argues that a civilization is a human achievement which embodies a culture and creates a world—that is, a way of seeing and structuring power and value. Hartt adduces seven characteristics of civilization as reasons for calling it a world. In the first four he describes civilization as (1) a comprehensive and pervasive ordering of human existence which (2) embraces both symbols and structures of meaning and inner appropriations of meaning, (3) extends through space and time, and (4) embodies the artistic and mundane achievements of a culture.

In the next three characteristics Hartt traces the development of the pathos of civilization. First, civilization is a way of "reckoning with ideality."[9] In other words, a civilization is an embodiment of human aspirations for the possible and the desirable which are generated as human beings wrestle with nature and history. But, secondly, because a civilization is concrete and finite, it cannot forever sustain human aspirations. Therefore, thirdly, since civilization cannot carry the weight which humans place upon it, civilization becomes "an object of continuous and inexhaustible concern."[10]

Here, then, is civilization as "world," as the pervasive, all-encompassing context for the lives of its members. But because it is concrete and finite, this "world" cannot suppress forever questions and anxieties about its ideals and its perdurability. As these questions and doubts arise, anxieties and fears spring first from concerns about civilization, about the humanly created world. Then, since civilization is an attempt to organize nature and history, these fears and anxieties about the humanly created world are attached to threatening cosmic powers and, in a self-promot-

---

[9]CC, 16. In this connection we have a nice example of Hartt's rhetoric:

High civilizations are prone to claim that their connections with ideality are normative for man as such. "Romanitas est Humanitas" is easily translated into German, English, American, Chinese, ad infinitum. Perhaps there is something to becoming civilized, i.e., to becoming human in a specific way, which automatically inflates the balloon of cosmic pretension. But perhaps this happens only when one is born on the winning side.

[10]Ibid., 17.

ing, self-protecting move, civilization presents itself as the one barrier between human being and cosmic extinction. Once this moment occurs, civilization becomes or produces a religion which deflects questions about its own being and enables its members to experience a time of happiness and optimism.

But no human creation, including a civilization, is immune to the vicissitudes of history and nature. Eventually, the questions and doubts arise at the very center of the "world." Then anxiety becomes acute, animating nostalgia and the passion for knowledge as control. At this point anxiety is not the possession merely of the sensitive artistic spirits, sage philosophers, keen social scientists, or insightful religious leaders of the age; now anxiety penetrates into the heart of civilization, into the common life, the "everyday world."

"Everyday world" is a crucial concept in Hartt's theological critique of culture. In his analysis of the human achievement of civilization as the embodiment of a culture which creates a world, the everyday world emerges as that which persistently and accurately expresses and determines a civilization's reading of the human situation. "Everyday world" expresses Hartt's concern to keep theology focused on the practicalities and actualities of life. It is his recognition that social expectation determines much of our lives, that a civilization teaches its members how "properly" to see the world.

In *The Restless Quest* Hartt further elucidates his understanding of the everyday world (which he there calls Q, for quotidian) by relating it to the natural world (N) and the ideal world (I).[11] In this analysis, Hartt shows that "N is the world upon whose routines Q tries to establish its own. . . . Thus, man must eat to live; that is a law of N. But in order to live he ought not to eat his brother; that

---

[11]*RQ*, 103-13. This analysis occurs in a chapter on "Secularity and the Transcendence of God" in which Hartt seeks to show "that the sense a Christian can discover in secularity is superior to the account a secularist provides of the same phenomenon" (97). See further discussion of Hartt's interpretation of secularity, below.

is a law of Q."[12] The everyday world and nature live in some tension. Nature is not always friendly, and everyday frequently expresses humanity's attempts to transcend nature.

The relationship of Q and N to I is complex. In relation to N, "I includes the possible and the desirable, the not-yet and the ought-to-be."[13] In relation to Q, I overarches and in various ways pervades the everyday world in the expectations which Q places upon its inhabitants. The ideal world may generate challenges to the routines of everyday, but even as it does Q attempts to stave it off by showing that I is merely an idealization of Q. Thus, everything claimed by I is already available in Q. Ultimately, then, I and Q are one world living in tension and anxiety, since "I is a set of idealizations of Q, and Q is a systematic response to the demands of I."[14]

Thus we arrive at a description of the human situation in which humans create Q in order to come to some terms with N. But as humans reflect upon Q and N and project what might have been or what might yet be, I presses in with questions about every achievement of Q.[15] As we have seen, a civilization may experience a time in which Q provides unquestioned guidance and comfort. Eventually, however, Q begins to breakdown; the questions springing from I thrust anxiety into the depths of everyday. But because

---

[12]Ibid., 104.
[13]Ibid.
[14]Ibid., 106.
[15]In CC, 213, Hartt describes the ideality of situation this way:

> The present condition of man must be graced with reflection upon what he may yet become within the boundaries of that social order, or at the very least upon what he might have been but for cruel chance. The latter is the ideality of the subjunctive contrary to fact and to historical likelihood; but it is not without its comfort. The former is the ideality held within the iron boundaries of the presuppositions of that civilization; and it is much more likely to satisfy the imagination if not to modify the behavior.

This analysis is developed in Hartt's christology where he shows how Jesus overcomes both the guilt which collapses the past into the present and the anxiety which collapses the future into the present. See above.

I is grounded in Q, even the ideal world promises no hope of transcendence. Everyday, trembling with agitations and anxieties, is the final end of civilization.

• "World" and Kingdom •

The process of concern, certainty and comfort, questions, anxiety, and breakdown is the "natural history" of civilization. But the Gospel of Jesus Christ reveals something more than N, Q, or I. The Gospel, in revealing the real shape of the world, also reveals the lies and illusions of everyday, the unreality of the ideal world, and humanity's proper relation to the natural world. In Jesus Christ the Kingdom of God brings the "natural history" of civilization under the redemptive judgment of God. Therefore, in order more fully to understand Hartt's conception of "world" we must look at it in relation to the Gospel of the Kingdom.

In the actuality, intelligibility, and dialectic of the Kingdom, the world is revealed as the object and arena of God's judgment and redemption.[16] God's judgment reveals the illusions of our worlds; God's redemption reveals the possibilities of our worlds. However, we must also remember that judgment and redemption are not two stages in God's work; they do not refer to two epochs in God's relationship to the world or to two different works of Christ. Rather, judgment and redemption, the disclosure of illusions and possibilities, are bound together in the revelation of the Kingdom of God in Jesus Christ. Therefore, any judgment of the illusions of culture is also an assertion about the real shape of the world; and any assertion about the real shape of the world is also judgment of our illusions. Thus, Hartt's interpretation of the Gospel in the preaching, person, and work of Jesus Christ is already judgment of illusions, a critique of culture, and the disclosure of God's redemption of creation.

---

[16]The pairing of object and arena is meant to reflect Hartt's claim that Jesus Christ participated fully in the human condition, i.e., in a world, without having his being exhausted by that participation.

The illusions of a world cannot be known truly to be illusions apart from the revelation of God in Jesus Christ. We can know the breakdown of a world, we can know the idealities which press upon it, we can know the anxieties and agitations which beset it, but we cannot know its illusions to be illusions until we see the shape of the real world revealed in the Kingdom of God. When we see the Kingdom, then the breakdown of civilization, its idealities, and its anxieties, are all shown to rest upon illusions about the human situation.

Since each civilization is a unique achievement, we cannot specify ahead of time which illusions are constitutive of a world. Some illusions may be present in several worlds across space and time; but again those cannot be identified prior to interpretation in the light of the Gospel. However, we can note that for Hartt "illusion" is a theological category. That is, "illusion" is anything which alienates humanity from God or from one another by misconstruing the situation of humanity.

In this light, all of Hartt's work is directed toward a single aim: to witness to the Kingdom of God and thereby to expose the illusions of a world in order to "save the present age."[17] To see in the Kingdom of God the shape of the real world and the illusions of our own creation is to see God's judgment of our world. But to see God's judgment, to see the Kingdom, is also to see God's redemption; judgment and redemption are given together in Jesus Christ. God's judgment, then, is not God's rejection of the world; rather, it is God's love for and redemption of the world which is God's creation.

Thus, the redemption of the world which is accomplished in Jesus Christ not only judges the illusions of "world," it also creates the possibilities in the world for the church to communicate the Gospel. "Possibilities" does not promise some future achievement of the aspirations of a civilization; nor does it draw in any other way upon the idealities of a civilization. Rather, "possibilities" denotes the conviction that the Kingdom is actually present and

---

[17]*RQ*, 49.

that every world can be addressed intelligibly and relevantly by the church's preaching.[18]

In his Christological essay Hartt shows how Jesus Christ overcomes the world.[19] This overcoming is the present actuality of the Kingdom of God, which breaks the power of our illusory worlds.[20] In breaking these powers, the Kingdom reveals that humanity can never cease to be God's creation and can never escape the reach of God's redemption.

Since the Kingdom is everlastingly actual, the church is everlastingly bound and enabled to proclaim the presence of the Kingdom in contemporary language. Since the Kingdom reveals God's redemption of the world as God's creation, the church cannot simply reject or denounce the world. Since the Kingdom reveals God's judgment of the world as humanity's creation, the church cannot simply accept or approve the world. In order for the church to fulfill her vocation, in order for the Gospel to be preached and the Kingdom to be witnessed, the church must continually assay civilization and the church's place in civilization. The purpose of this theological critique of culture is to distinguish the good creations from the evil, the things which serve the Kingdom of God from those which serve the kingdom of death, in order that the Gospel may be preached intelligibly—the Kingdom witnessed and served—in every aspect of the church's life. This is the calling which is served by theology as cultural critique.

• Hartt's Critique of Culture •

Theology of culture, according to Hartt, should always be engaged in cultural critique no matter what its focal point. For example, when the Gospel of Jesus Christ is in focus, culture is at the same time being interpreted. And any development of ecclesi-

---

[18]See 91-94.

[19]CC, 165-230.

[20]In this connection see the works of Hendrikus Berkhof, *Christ and the Powers* (Scottdale PA: Herald Press, 1962), and John Howard Yoder, *The Politics of Jesus. Vicit Agnus Noster* (Grand Rapids: Eerdmans, 1972) chap. 8.

ology also requires attention to the cultural situation. However, although theology should always be engaged in a critique of culture, this critique can operate at many different levels.

Theological critique of culture may seek to discern where a civilization is in the natural history which Hartt has described. Is a civilization on the ascent? Is it providing cosmic comfort and happiness for its members? Is it being questioned? Is it breaking down?

Theological critique of culture may seek to discern the specific creations, attitudes, and values which mark a culture. Here cultural critique is guided by the revelation of God and the human situation in the Gospel of Jesus Christ. What are the culture's images of humanity? What categories does it apply to humanity? How does it construe the human situation? What are its images for God? How does it construe the God-human relationship?

Theology of culture may examine the everyday world, the artistic expressions of a culture, the economic life, politics, and many other aspects in order to discern the proper theological critique of culture. But through all of its work, the purpose of theology of culture will be to enable the church to witness to the Kingdom which is the judgment and redemption of God's creation.

Hartt's theological critique of culture operates on all of these levels as he subjects "American culture" to the judgment and redemption of the Gospel. But on Hartt's own understanding, the work of theology as cultural critique is never-ending; theology must continually be assaying culture and church in the light of the Kingdom. As a culture changes, theology is presented with new challenges, new threats, new possibilities. Therefore, Hartt's critique of culture twenty years ago should itself be assayed for its continuing value; but that is a full-length project and not the one at hand. Moreover, Hartt's whole project is a critique of the life of the church and its vocation in the "Christian civilization" which is American culture.[21] So I will not be able to do his account justice

---

[21]This is true not only of CC, but also of Hartt's other books, articles, and reviews. In *TCU* (179-204) he analyzes the impact on America of the liturgical-political orders of ancient Israel, Greece, the Puritans, and William Shakespeare.

in these few pages. What I will do is delineate some of the features of his critique of culture that may serve to guide our own work.

Hartt's critique of American culture operates at a fairly general level. He places American culture within "Christian civilization" and offers several lines of critique which could apply to other "cultures" within the Western World, and perhaps beyond. This characteristic does not vitiate Hartt's critique. Perhaps it implies the conviction that theology renders a general critique which each church then renders concrete and local in its witness to the Kingdom.

The Age of Anxiety. Hartt identifies the place of our civilization in its natural history as the age of anxiety. In other words, our civilization no longer provides us with an everyday that works. Hartt draws on art, science, and philosophy to show that "our anxiety is ontological, it reaches, that is, into the depths of contemporary life."[22] Thus, our worries about success are no longer connected merely with achieving or holding onto success, our anxiety now concerns whether success matters at all. As persons seek to resist attacks of anxiety, they are further threatened by "fragmentation" in our society: "the demands for total loyalty made by powerful conflicting forces in contemporary civilization, rather than the simple fact of multiple goals and standards."[23] Added to this is the depersonalization of humanity: "everywhere mass man looks the prospects are roughly similar: he is going to be engineered, manipulated, slickered, flummoxed, and cut to standard measurements."[24]

In *LI* and in many reviews he delineates the crisis of the image of humanity in modern literature. Among his insights here is the distinction between normlessness and aimlessness (see "The Loss of Normativeness," a review of five novels in *The Christian Scholar* 47 [Summer 1964]: 176-83). In *The Critique of Modernity* he draws out the different effects of covenant and contract upon our culture. In *RQ* he offers several interpretations of secularity in contemporary culture.

[22]*CC*, 18-19.

[23]Ibid., 23.

[24]Ibid., 24. Hartt's descriptions of fragmentation and depersonalization anticipate many of the features of Alasdair MacIntyre's account of the failure of the Enlightenment project in *After Virtue* (Notre Dame IN: University of Notre Dame Press, 1981) and various accounts of the postmodern condition.

As our society confronts these anxieties, art, science, and philosophy can diagnose the anxieties, heighten awareness of them, and rail against them. When anxiety brings civilization to the point of becoming or producing a religion, even the church may become a part of the anxiety of everyday as religion and piety are assimilated to culture.[25] Art, in its many forms, may rebel against everyday and at its best creates a world which expresses judgment upon everyday, thus heightening anxiety with truth. Science, too, both physical and social, lays claim to special perspective on and unique knowledge of everyday and continually confronts us with the fragility of our world. Philosophy, and not only existentialist varieties, descries the anxieties of our world which are manifested in convictions of the meaninglessness and alienation of the human condition.

But although art, science, and philosophy can diagnose anxiety, heighten awareness of it, and rail against it, they cannot overcome anxiety. Art, science, and philosophy are part of everyday. They may create images, visions, and conceptual schemes which reveal in new and unexpected ways the anxieties of a civilization, but they cannot transcend everyday except by appeal to ideality—which is simply another form of everyday. Indeed, Hartt shows that while art, science, and philosophy have done much to identify the anxiety of our age, they have also contributed much to our anxiety.[26] Thus, the anxieties of our own civilization are further exacerbated "by the discovery of civilization's global character. The critic of civilization has no place to stand to do his work, to speak his piece, except within the object he is judging. He has no critical appliances except the values of the order he wishes to appraise."[27] There is no redemption, no salvation from within, and there is nothing outside. There is only the kingdom of sin and death.

By identifying ours as an age of anxiety, Hartt places our civilization at the point of breakdown. At this point in its natural

---

[25]Hartt sees much "theology of culture" as responsible for this assimilation of religion to everyday. See *CC*, 28, 38.

[26]*CC*, 25-39.

[27]Ibid., 40.

history, civilization often calls upon the resources of religion which have been assimilated to cultural piety. In our civilization, the church has provided many resources for the piety of civilization. Culture Christianity has reinforced the claims of everyday. When a citizen fails to meet the demands of everyday the church provides a means for the "sinner" to have a change of heart—that is, a change in emotional state so that he or she can get back to the demands of everyday. But seldom is the "sinner" led to a change of heart which is a change of loyalty—that is, a commitment to the demands of the Kingdom of God over and above the demands of everyday, of civilization. The church also provides the means for justifying the order of civilization, but seldom means for its guidance. In spite of these efforts (and in part because of them), the piety of civilization—and culture Christianity—trembles with the anxieties of everyday. Even as they seek to justify everyday and assuage guilt, they cannot stave off anxiety.[28]

Thus, the illusions and breakdown of civilization are exposed by the anxiety of everyday. The inhabitants of everyday reach a point of disillusionment, of disenchantment. But their anxiety shows that there is yet further disillusionment to be achieved. The anxiety of everyday is not the final disillusionment, because it rest upon a deeper illusion.

The deepest illusion which fuels humanity's anxiety and alienation is the belief that human being is founded in human civilization or it is founded nowhere. Thus, as a civilization which has been entrusted with humanity begins to crumble, humanity is faced with the prospect of nothingness, of nonbeing. In this situation, humanity naturally questions the "ontology" of a civilization. But the suspicion that humanity is founded in civilization or it is founded in nothing is itself the final illusion. The good news of Jesus Christ, the revelation of the Kingdom, the message of the faithful church, and the aim of theology as cultural critique, is to expose this final illusion in the light of the revelation of humanity's being in God's creation and redemption.

---

[28]Ibid., 42-47.

Human Being as History. Hartt's conception of theology as cultural critique requires the church faithfully to witness to the actuality of God's Kingdom in ways intelligible to a world marked by the anxieties Hartt has described. To accomplish this task, the church cannot simply repeat the parables of Jesus, the assertions of the letter to the Colossians, or the formulas of Nicea and Chalcedon. In order to be faithful to its commission in our world, the church must endure a "categorial revolution" as it lays hold of the possibilities in the world for witnessing to the everlastingly actual Kingdom come in Jesus Christ.

We cannot specify a method by which the church lays hold of any of the possibilities for witness prior to the actual practice of witnessing, prior to the categorial revolution which the church undergoes. What can be specified are the conditions under which the church may be faithful and relevant. The conditions specified by Hartt were examined in the previous chapter and found to be fruitful, though in need of supplementation. Here we will examine how Hartt lays hold of the historicizing of humanity in order to communicate the Gospel.

The major factor giving rise to the anxieties of our civilization, says Hartt, is

> the philosophical-scientific "historicizing" of man's being. . . . The historicizing of man's being means that concrete human existence is fully absorbed into the fabric and process of the civilization in which persons appear and live. It seems to follow from this (though actually it is part of the viewpoint) that man has no history as such; and so ceases to exist as such. Essential human being is thereafter parceled out to the multitudinous particular human communities and their cultures, each of which is called human for purposes of cataloguing.[29]

---

[29]Ibid. Hartt attacked this historicism and its destruction of the human early in his career. See "The Situation of the Believer" in *Faith and Ethics*, 225-44, where he argues, against one trend in H. Richard Niebuhr's thought, "that persons cannot be resolved or reduced into nexus of relations, for then the relations are left without ground and without meaning" (243). Hartt's argument here is consonant with his later work, since the argument turns on the logic of the

With this analysis Hartt sets history as the major focus for a theological critique of our civilization and for the preaching of the Gospel in our world. We should not lose sight of the impact of this historicizing on the anxieties which beset everyday. The "problem of history" is not an abstract, intellectual issue; it is not a methodological challenge. The problem of history pervades the human situation as it is construed by our civilization.[30]

Hartt expounds four categories of history with which our "world" of human creation confronts the witnessing church. He does not view these four as exhaustive of the historicizing of humanity in our culture, but he does expect them to be a way in which the church can confront the "mind of the age" and expose the illusions of that mind through a theological critique of culture.[31]

The first category confronted by the church and the last to be let go by the world is *fate*:

When a man says fate, he confesses that he is a meaningless moment in a cosmos perfectly unfeeling in all its members except for the human heart. Worlds and men arise and pass away in response to cosmic rhythms we cannot call either good or evil. In all of the great events wherein souls are lost or gained, we are

---

Christian belief in revelation: "To *have* a perspective is not to *be* one. To apprehend Revelation, to be caught up in a dialogue with God, is to be a real terminal existent. What God 'sees' when he beholds us, is not an appearance or 'projection' of himself, but an other and an order of others. When he addresses one of these others, he addresses someone other than himself" (242). Hartt thinks that another trend, Niebuhr's "social existentialism" (*Christ and Culture*, 241-49), concurs with Hartt's analysis of the situation of the believer.

[30]In this chapter we will be concerned with the historicality of human being. In chap. 6 we will consider how to overcome alien views of history that have infected theological method.

[31]Ibid., 232. Although I will restrict the discussion to one chapter in Hartt's work, his entire *ouvre* could be read as an elucidation of the demands the Gospel makes upon history.

but pawns of mighty forces so dark, silent, and unheeding we cannot call them purpose.[32]

Against the understanding of history as fate the Gospel discloses history as destiny.

In the Gospel, human destiny is seen, like the notion of fate, to be a recognition that time as mere succession does not make humanity; history, the "concrete moment" makes humanity.[33] However, unlike fate, which sees humanity's teleology as determined by the cosmos, destiny identifies humanity as creatures who participate *"by choice* in a teleological order which embraces the cosmos but cannot be learned from the cosmos."[34] Like fate, destiny sees history as "the momentous and memorable rather than the trivial and commonplace." Unlike fate, which locates necessity in the future as accomplished fact, destiny locates necessity *"in the call of God to life in the community of His creation. Man can be only what God calls him to become."*[35] This means that creative use of human powers can only be found in serving the Kingdom of God. The call of God reveals to humanity the necessity of serving God alone. But the Kingdom also reveals that serving God is not the destruction of one's humanity but its fulfillment.

By so locating necessity, this understanding of destiny also shows that the proper way to relate the Kingdom of God to the rise and fall of the kingdoms of earth is in the "struggle to reconcile the necessity inherent in teleological order with the fierce independence of contingent events."[36] Finally, unlike fate, which teaches despair as the appropriate disposition toward history (and occasionally produces the tragic-heroic), human destiny revealed in the Gospel teaches joy as the appropriate disposition. All that the past has brought and all that the future can bring has been

---

[32]Ibid., 234.

[33]Here Hartt draws on his rejection of linear and cyclical views of time in favor of "periodicity." See *CC*, 142-44.

[34]Ibid., 235.

[35]Ibid., 237; his emphasis.

[36]Ibid., 238-39.

shown in Jesus Christ to participate in the Kingdom which is human destiny.

The second category of history encountered by the witnessing church is the *demonic*. The success of the doctrine of fate results in the denial of the devil, of the demonic as cosmic powers which more and less determine history. Thereafter, the demonic becomes identified with the destructive spirit and evil in humankind, particularly as it is manifested in one's adversaries. Now we wrestle only against flesh and blood, and the evil they perpetrate must be overcome: "every weapon must be turned upon that hideous strength, cunning must be met with greater cunning, violence with greater violence, lies with greater lies. Evil must be overcome with its own instruments, or one has failed to keep faith—with the good!"[37] Since the Kingdom reveals the unity of God and humanity, we are unfaithful witnesses if we seek to sunder that community.[38]

Against the denial of the demonic and the consequent rise of diabolism, Christianity takes the demonic seriously by proclaiming the victory of Jesus Christ over the demonic. The Gospel gives no explanation of the origin of the demonic. However, the Gospel does reveal that the powers of darkness are the powers of non-being, they are anticreation. Their weapons are deceit and guile; they enter human history through the illusions which hold humanity captive. These powers exacerbate alienation, deepening and widening the separation of humanity from God and from one another.

As Hartt shows, one of the illusions perpetrated by the denial of the powers of darkness is the conviction that human beings are

---

[37]Ibid. 243. Although Hartt does not extend this discussion further, this is one of the most compelling expositions I know of the logic of Christian nonresistance and martyrdom.

[38]Hartt's cautionary statements about the logic of one particular line of argument from Jesus' command that we love our enemies (CC, 102-105) does not vitiate this claim. In the earlier discussion Hartt was simply demonstrating the limitations of strict logical inference. For further development of Christian "pacifism" along the lines identified above see the writings of John Howard Yoder and Stanley Hauerwas.

demonic. This conviction leads to violence and a violation of the church's witness to the Kingdom. The demonic can also lead in another way to the church's abdication of her mission. When the demonic is attached to a human community, then "they" are unrighteous, and we must protect our righteousness by withdrawing from them.[39] Such withdrawal is not the rhythm of going out and return that Hartt commends to the church; it is a denial of the human community as God's creation and redemption and is, therefore, a betrayal of the Gospel. The Gospel discloses this "diabolism" as an illusion by revealing that humanity is the community created and redeemed by God; only God has the power to sunder the human community. The church, therefore, is bound to proclaim the Gospel to all humanity, all nations, without fear—and without favor.

In the Gospel, human history is shown to be, not the story of humanity wrestling alone with the demonic, not the story of a righteous race versus an unrighteous race, but rather the story of human encounter with the judgment and redemption of God. In Jesus Christ, God has revealed that humanity is created to be a community; and in Jesus Christ God creates that community. History, then, is neither fated nor diabolical; it is revealed by the Gospel to be the place where humanity enters the Kingdom of God.

The third category of modern historical consciousness with which the church must wrestle is the *end*. Our culture has done much to create illusions regarding the end of a human life and the end of the human race.[40] We develop ritualistic, philosophical, and scientific controls to sustain our illusions. As humanity lives in the present and anticipates the end, humanity's "being is stretched

---

[39]See *CC*, 247-48.

[40]The classic analysis of these illusions is Ernst Becker, *The Denial of Death* (New York: Free Press, 1973). A fascinating expression of the illusion that humanity holds its fate in its own hands is Jonathan Schell, *The Fate of the Earth* (New York: Alfred A. Knopf, 1982). See Stanley Hauerwas's exposure of Schell's illusions in Stanley Hauerwas, *Against the Nations: War and Survival in a Liberal Society* (Minneapolis: Winston Press, 1985), 160-68.

between the envisagement of an end and the realization of the end envisaged. Envisagement brings together the present and the future. Realization brings together the present and the past."[41] Thus, how one envisages the end greatly affects how one shapes life in the present.

Our own culture seems to envision the end as the end, as nothing, as the termination of time and of the life of the world. Since the end lacks value, is void of significance, our culture harbors the deep suspicion that the process itself is void of value. Thus, the shape of life in the present also lacks value. Anxiety here reaches its depths: is all of life, all of humanity, an illusion? In the protests of our culture against such a conclusion, the Christian sees the inextinguishable light of God's creation and redemption.

Against this view of the end, the Gospel declares Jesus Christ to be the revelation of the end of time. Jesus Christ is the end of time as the revelation of the supreme value of the whole process. Through Jesus Christ God reveals the consummation of the human story. Death is shown properly to be a part of the process, but not the last word, not the final end of humanity.

When one envisages the termination of time, the consummation of humanity in Jesus Christ, one then shapes life in relation to that end. Now life can be lived joyfully. Now we know the truth of our being; we can give ourselves away to others because our worth, our being, is assured in the Kingdom of God. This life can be realized in actual and proper relation to Jesus Christ only through the presence of the Holy Spirit. Through the gifts of the Holy Spirit called hope, love, and joy, one realizes now the end which is envisaged in Jesus Christ. And to live in that hope, love, and joy is to participate in the Kingdom of God here and now.

In the Gospel, Jesus Christ is also revealed as the consummation of history: "from him we learn how to be historical without being the creatures of history."[42] Being "historical" means that a human life is the acquisition of an essence, a project which "is

---

[41]CC, 250.
[42]Ibid., 253.

stretched over time rather than merely pursued in time."[43] When the historicality of human being is captured by illusion and human being is seen also as creation of history, then the anxieties and uncertainties which attend the acquisition of essence seem insoluble—rage, denial, despair, become the modes of human expression. But Jesus Christ also reveals that human being is not the creation of history; human being is God's creation realized in history.[44] And in God's Kingdom of creation and redemption, the true end of human life has become everlastingly actual. When human life is drawn into this Kingdom, "acquisition of an essence," that is, realizing one's God-created humanity by participating in the Kingdom of God, means a life of joy and freedom.

The final category of which the preaching church must give an account is *providence*. In American culture providence "has been crossbred with fate, fortune, sheer luck, self-righteousness, and a certain naive optimism of outlook characteristic of American civilization."[45] Theological accounts of providence have almost always, under the impact of Kantian philosophy and scientific cosmologies, subsumed any providential care of the cosmos under an account of God's providence in history.[46]

---

[43]Ibid., 254-55. For what Hartt means by essence see above, 65-70, and *CC*, 188-92.

[44]The seminal article by Stephen Crites, "The Narrative Quality of Experience," *Journal of the American Academy of Religion* 39/3 (September 1971): 291-311, develops Hartt's insights into human life as historical. However, Crites gives an account of human being as history that does not depend upon the revelation of Jesus Christ. Thus, he gives an account of human being as history, but does not add to that the insight that we are God's creation, not the creatures of history. In Hartt's view, the true narrative of human life is given only in Jesus Christ. For development of that side of Hartt (in ways with which Hartt would have some disagreement), see Stanley Hauerwas, *A Community of Character*, 111-52, and *The Peaceable Kingdom*, 35-49.

[45]Ibid., 257.

[46]James Gustafson's recent work, however, seems to move in the other direction. Gustafson is "historicist," but his fundamental concern is not with the history of humanity, but with the history of nature. Thus, the natural sciences set the limits for what can be affirmed theologically. See James M. Gustafson, *Ethics from a Theocentric Perspective. Volume One: Theology and Ethics* (Chicago: University

In the Gospel, Jesus Christ is the revelation of God's providence in two distinct realms, history and cosmos. Jesus Christ reveals this all-governing providence when as an historical person he also reveals being and good; he is the revelation of the reason of history and of the cosmos. The Kingdom of God is not the overcoming of cosmos by history; nor is it the overcoming of history by cosmos. Rather, the Kingdom of God is the proper end of both history and cosmos. This proper dialectic of creation and redemption, of cosmos and history, is one crucial element in Hartt's account of the preaching, person and work of Jesus Christ.

This dialectic of the Kingdom, when held in proper tension, overcomes several dangerous tendencies in theology. First, it exposes as false any eschatology which seeks to destroy creation, being and good, in the name of a good supposed to be available only at the end of history. Secondly, it exposes as false any reduction of history to mere "consent to being"; history is also the overcoming of illusion and alienation. Thirdly, it exposes the destructive powers of the world as parasitic, as demonic, as historical rather than cosmic.

In the Gospel, human being is revealed to be historical but not history's creation. History is the story of humanity's relationship to the Creator. The story is full of pathos, but in the Gospel of Jesus Christ the end of the story, the consummation is shown to be beyond the deepest longing, richer than the wildest dreams. And that Kingdom is with us now; we participate in it now through the gift of the Holy Spirit. The right preaching of the Kingdom of God revealed in Jesus Christ shatters the "world" which holds us in bondage to history-as-fate and shows that in history-as-destiny we are apprehended by the freedom and love for which we were created.

Images of Humanity. All of Hartt's theological critique of culture may be viewed as a struggle for the rebirth of the image of humanity as created and redeemed by God. In his critique of the historicizing of humanity's being, he establishes humanity as the

---

of Chicago Press, 1981) esp. 251-52.

creation of God not of history, and shows how properly to view humanity's historicality. His critique of secularity argues powerfully for the Christian affirmation of divine-human community as God's purpose. And his critique of modernity exposes the anti-human characteristics of corporation in comparison to the longing for community.

In *The Lost Image of Man*, Hartt delineates ways in which Western culture has abandoned the images of humanity present in its heritage. Hartt develops his argument by adducing the works of the best contemporary writers.[47] By reference to Joyce and Hemingway, Hartt describes the loss of the epic image. We have fragments of the image expressed in accounts of war, in the anti-conventional hero, in Christ images, and in the Communist revolutionary. But all of these fail as epic images because none claims engagement with the determinative powers of existence. The prime characteristic of war is its pointlessness: the anticonventional hero saves only himself; the Christ image is broken, impotent; the revolutionary is the product of powers.

By reference to Faulkner and Camus, Hartt traces the shattering of the dream of innocence. Our culture, says Hartt, confuses innocence and purity. Innocence supposes a world congenial to one's fulfillment and "a vagueness of boundary between one's own being and other beings."[48] Once lost, innocence is irrecoverable. Purity, on the other hand, is freedom from guilt. If lost, purity can be recovered through right relationship to the good. When innocence and purity are seen as one, then the loss of innocence is the loss of purity and humanity is condemned to live in guilt.

By reference to Lawrence, Styron, Durrell, and Alberto Moravia, Hartt describes three stages in the travail of erotic man. From Lawrence's celebration of erotic love as the expression of true human existence, Hartt traces the decline of erotic love through its subjection to fate in Styron's *Lie Down in Darkness*, to

---

[47]*LI*, 12-37. Hartt uses "man" inclusively at times, but his analysis is also sometimes exclusively focused on the male sex. Since I am here seeking to exposit Hartt, I will follow his usage.

[48]Ibid., 39.

Durrell's exposure of the suffering and despair it brings. In Moravia's *The Empty Canvas*, Hartt finds both a cold, clinical demystification of sexual love and a hint of the recovery of love as being in the human community.

By reference to Steinbeck, Koestler, Camus, Paton, and Faulkner, Hartt identifies the vicissitudes of eschatological man. Steinbeck's *In Dubious Battle* exposes the optimistic-realistic eschatology of Marxism. In the novel, the cause of the classless, peaceful community is served through violence and the destruction of persons. Koestler's *Darkness at Noon* powerfully witnesses the "violent recoil against the soul-destroying image of Marxist historical optimism," by telling the story of the torture and execution of an old Bolshevik leader.[49] Camus' *The Plague* witnesses the recoil against eschatological man, not just Marxist man, and seeks to erase eschatological hope from the modern scene—in spite of Marxism and Scientism we are still plague infected.

As the eschatological image dies, so also does the image of the Kingdom of God, the divine-human community. Hartt finds a requiem for this image in Paton's *Cry the Beloved Country*. In Stephen Kumalo, eschatological man is "certified and validated."[50] Kumalo hopes for the Kingdom of God. If that hope is not fulfilled historically in Kumalo's lifetime, it can still be fulfilled ethically through Kumalo's love for his enemies. And even if Kumalo fails to love his enemies the Kingdom can be witnessed to by his confession of failure.[51]

Other Aspects of Culture. Although Hartt's major cultural critique is directed toward the historicizing of human being, several other aspects of culture also receive attention in his work.

---

[49]Ibid., 76.

[50]Ibid., 87.

[51]What I find striking in this account is the absence of the church. It seems to me that Kumalo's witness to the Kingdom and the ethical fulfillment of his hope requires the church. There is a profound similarity between the absence of church and the tragedy of Kumalo in Paton's novel and the same elements in Bonhoeffer's life as described in James William McClendon's *Ethics*, 187-208.

In *The Restless Quest*, Hartt analyzes "Secularity and the Transcendence of God."[52] Secularity, he argues, is a plea for human community in response to religion that sets God transcendent over against humanity. On this interpretation, the impulse of secularity is right. But the fulfillment of that aspiration for human community is found, not in the rejection of God transcendent, but in relation to God in Jesus Christ who is the revelation of God and the human situation. In Jesus Christ humanity is brought into divine-human community without any diminishing of humanity. In Jesus Christ, God transcendent pledges the fulfillment of human aspiration for community. Secularity, then, is a rebuke to Christians who are not witnessing and serving the Kingdom of God. The proper response, however, is not to abandon faith in God transcendent; the proper response is better to practice that faith.[53]

In *The Critique of Modernity*, Hartt offers his most material critique of culture by analyzing "modernity" as a shift from community to corporation, from covenant to contract.[54] Hartt draws on themes present in his other work—such as history, destiny, hope—in order to suggest a critique of modernity that springs from the "grass roots" and, in contrast to the "masters of suspicion," draws on moral values in order to mount a critique.

In Hartt's analysis, modernity is not synonymous with contemporary culture. Rather, at the grass roots modernity is seen in the turn from community to corporation. The corporation is a social organization marked by rationality, efficiency, utility, technique, and "impersonality combined with pseudoindividuality."[55] The corporation thrives on a view of the real world as the arena in which there is no human community, there are only individuals competing for power and success, each for him or herself.

---

[52]*RQ*, 97-113.

[53]See *RQ*, 113.

[54]Julian N. Hartt, Ray L. Hart, and Robert Scharlemann, *The Critique of Modernity: Theological Reflections on Contemporary Culture* (Charlottesville: University Press of Virginia) 1-33; cf. his summary of the essay, xvi-xvii.

[55]Ibid., 20.

Hartt is content in this essay simply to expose the differences between community and corporation. His concern is analysis; he does not mount a full-scale theological critique of modernity. However, from his other writings we can know that the characteristics of modernity displayed in the corporation are the creation of human illusion about the human situation. Although the corporation created by such illusion is an artificial institution, its powers over human existence are real enough. But Hartt does not see the corporation dominating the future. Rather, he sees corporation and community living in tension as humanity continues to aspire in fitful and mistaken ways for that Kingdom revealed in Jesus Christ.

• Conclusion •

In this chapter, we have examined Hartt's critique of the "world." Behind and within this critique lies the

> conviction that Christian theology is improperly done only at the end—or in homiletical forays into the arts along the way—to consider the cultural situation of faith. Theology of culture seeks to relocate and reestablish the very foundations and form of Christian theology. It is not enough for culture to appear somewhere in theological systems as a topic of high importance. Theology proper must begin with the analysis of culture or it will prove to be systematically meaningless.[56]

Given Hartt's claims and his faithfulness to them, we must recognize that from beginning to end his theology is an enactment of this conviction.

Throughout Hartt's critique of culture, his concern is the rebirth of the image of the Kingdom of God, the divine-human community, as revealed in the Gospel of Jesus Christ, so that we may discern the present actuality of the Kingdom and participate in it. In his critique of the historicizing of humanity, Hartt seeks the restoration of the image of humanity as God's creation and redemption. History is thereby an aspect of humanity's being, but

---

[56]CC, xviii.

only as history belongs to God. Hartt's critique of secularity and modernity shows the distortions and illusions which attend human aspiration for community and seeks to direct that aspiration toward the Kingdom witnessed to in the Gospel of Jesus Christ. Finally, Hartt, in his delineation of the loss of the images of humanity which have formed our culture, points, sometimes implicitly, sometimes explicitly, toward the Gospel of the Kingdom.

In this work the Gospel serves as revelation, foundation, and authority for theology as cultural critique. The "world" serves as a "source" for theology only as it is subjected to the critique of the Kingdom revealed in the Gospel. Because of the actuality of the Kingdom, theological critique of culture is bound to expose the illusions and unreality of culture. Because of the intelligibility of the Kingdom, theological critique of culture must attend to its particular civilization, its particular world. Because of the dialectic of creation and redemption, this critique of culture must discern the evil and the good, the illusions and the truths, the unreality and the reality, in the world.

Thus, the faithful church cannot find its ease by simply rejecting the world. Neither can the church simply accept and approve the world. The faithful church is bound to the everlasting tension of being in the world but not of the world as the church fulfills her vocation to witness to and serve the Kingdom which is the judgment of all our illusions and alienation and the fulfillment of all our hopes and aspirations.

In all of his analysis, Hartt never gives a strict definition of culture or world; nor does he explicitly position himself in relation to the debates about defining culture and world. This omission is, I think, deliberate; and it is one strength of Hartt's work. Since Hartt shows his awareness of the debates by indirectly addressing the debate about culture and world at many points, his not taking up a position must be deliberate. Hartt deliberately refuses to strictly define culture and world because he recognizes that any such definition becomes blinders which restrict vision of the world to that definition. Thus, for example, identifying world as a linguistic system tends toward denying other aspects of world, such as its material conditions. For Hartt, world is a systematic theological concern, but its form and meaning (to work with the language we have) can only be discerned ad hoc, by seeing the world in the light of the Gospel. This is the strength of Hartt's openness in construing the world: every aspect of world is to be brought into the light of the Gospel by theology as cultural critique.

Since Hartt's critique of the world is complex and interwoven with all of his theology, it is one of the most fertile areas of his theology for further research. At every point, Hartt's critique makes connections with contemporary debates. Up to now I have avoided the pedantry of noting every such possibility. I will now risk pedantry by briefly suggesting some directions for further engagement with Hartt's critique.[57]

First, if theological approaches to culture may be roughly characterized as apologetic, kerygmatic, or liberative, Hartt offers a complex alternative. Since Hartt's relation to liberation theology is latent, we will consider it briefly. The "theology of revolution" is the theology, with which Hartt contends, that most closely resembles some aspects of liberation theology.[58] As usual, Hartt does not name his subjects in his critique of this theology. For the most part, he is concerned with the revolutionary theology that attended the social upheavals of the 1960s in the U.S. His critique centers on the misuse of power, and the illusory substitution of humanly created institutions for the kingdom of God. Here, also, Hartt's criticisms of the ideal and of "propheticism" are appropriate wherever liberation theology can be shown to base its critique in something other than the actual, intelligible, and dialectical Kingdom of God. However, since Hartt's critique is clearly situated within the political history of the United States, any application of his critique to liberation theology would have to be considerably nuanced.

---

[57]In what follows, I will focus on theological positions. Hartt could also be profitably related to other approaches to culture. He incorporates materialist concerns, language, ideology, the everyday, and other broad issues into his account in ways that are quite prescient and illuminating. I hope to pursue such a comparison at another time.

[58]*RQ*, chaps. 4 and 7-9; *CC*, chap. 18.

Although complex, Hartt's relationship to apologetic and kerygmatic theology is more straightforward. If, for the moment, we take Tillich and his "method of correlation" as representative of the apologetic approach, Hartt differs significantly. Although Hartt's approach may be systematically apologetic in its call for theology to be concerned with culture from beginning to end, his interpretation of particular cultural artefacts is *ad hoc*. In place of correlation, Hartt offers "critique," rooted in the Kingdom of God. Although Hartt's theology is ontological, ontology does not displace theology as, according to Hartt, it does in Tillich's theology.[59] Finally, in contrast to Tillich's connection of theology of culture to "high art," Hartt connects theology of culture to everyday life.[60]

Although Barth is often identified as "kerygmatic" in his approach to culture, reconsiderations of his theology, along with some other factors, make H. R. Niebuhr's theology a more illuminating representative of kerygmatic theology for comparison.[61] Since preaching plays such a central role in Hartt's theology, his relationship to kerygmatic theology requires some development.

At a number of points, Hartt makes rather harsh statements about "confessionalist theology."[62] Hartt does not identify his opponent in these passages, but in a passing comment in another essay, he asserts that Niebuhr's objective in *The Meaning of Revelation* is "to provide a philosophical foundation and warrant for a confessionalist method in theology."[63] This rejection of "confessionalism" is directly tied to Hartt's critique of culture.

---

[59]See the third of Hartt's Nathaniel Taylor Lectures, "Onto-theology and the End of Salvation History," Yale Divinity School, 1982.

[60]Somewhat contrary to this claim, see the recent article, Kelton Cobb, "Reconsidering the Status of Popular Culture in Tillich's Theology of Culture," *Journal of the American Academy of Religion* 63/1 (Spring 1995): 53-84.

[61]For Hartt's criticisms of Barth and of retrievals of Barth's theology, esp. that of Hans Frei, see the next chapter, s.v. "Asserting the Truth."

[62]*RQ*, 14-16; *TMI*, 171-84. See my further discussion of these passages in the next chapter, under "Asserting the Truth."

[63]Julian Hartt, "Austin Farrer as Philosophical Theologian," in *For God and Clarity: New Essays in Honor of Austin Farrer*, ed. Jeffrey C. Eaton and Ann Loades (Allison Park PA: Pickwick Publications, 1983) 3.

In the previous chapter, I noted that Hartt's theology contains elements of most of Niebuhr's Christ-and-culture typology. This is due to his avoidance of Niebuhr's "monolithic" view of culture.[64] If culture is treated as monolithic, then we must chose *one* approach to culture. Hartt, however, views culture as a complex—in the light of the Gospel, some aspects of culture may be affirmed, others rejected, others transformed, still others ruled from above. As a result, the church may not simply address the culture or preach to it, the church must also argue with the culture. For Hartt, there are theological warrants for this approach in the reality, dialectic, and intelligibility of the Kingdom, but there are no a priori or universal specifications about what "points of contact" there may be.

So, in relation to apologetic and kerygmatic theology, Hartt's approach reveals something more complex. The great error toward which apologetic theology tends is the assumption that the point of contact between the Gospel and the world is always the same. The great error toward which kerygmatic theology tends is the assumption that since there is no universal point of contact, there is no point of contact. Hartt's theology avoids both errors, gives theological warrant for such avoidance, and develops a critique of the world with great sophistication and insight.

In a profoundly insightful review of "The Theological Situation After Fifty Years," Hartt, after analyzing various options in theology, argues that "a cosmological theology offers the richest promise of making the right address to the actual religious situation."[65] By "cosmological theology," Hartt means a theology that "Is concerned with realities disclosed actively in experience but commonly misunderstood and misappropriated in everyday life."[66] He goes on to argue that

---

[64]See John Howard Yoder's perceptive analysis of Niebuhr's monolithic view of culture in *Authentic Transformation*.

[65]Julian N. Hartt, "The Theological Situation After Fifty Years," *Yale Review* 51 (Autumn 1961): 75-101. The "fifty years" refers to the time between the founding of the *Yale Review* and the issue in question.

[66]Ibid., 98.

the time is ripe for the expression in force of the theological critique of the religious situation; critique inspired and designed to reconstruct experience, rather than to demonstrate by dialectical footwork the ultimate triumph of modernity over the errors of the past.[67]

In his analysis of the religious situation, his critique of everyday life, and his interpretation of the world, Hartt reconstructs human experience and the world in the light of the Gospel of Jesus Christ. In so doing, he demonstrates the richness of a "cosmological theology" that exemplifies theology as cultural critique.

---

[67]Ibid., 99. For Hartt's further criticism of "dialectical footwork," see his "Dialectic, Analysis, and Empirical Generalization in Theology," and William Wilson, "A Different Method; A Different Case."

Chapter 6

The Achievement of Julian Hartt

Some theologians feel that "the Christian thing" is either a story or it is nothing that can speak to contemporary sensibility. This is a counsel of despair. The New Testament faith is not just a story. It is also a strenuous effort to show how the import of the story must be made out: not only understood but, above all, appropriated. That requires theological work. Moreover, both as story and as theology the Christian faith has now, and has always had, to compete with other stories and other theologies. So I think it is a fundamental and far-reaching mistake to suppose that telling the story is the whole thing. What one makes of the world and of one's own existence on the strength of the story: that is the payoff. That is what real and decisive case making is.[1]

In the previous chapters I have sought to elucidate Julian Hartt's work under the rubrics of Gospel, church, and world. My purpose in elucidating Hartt's understanding of these three concepts has not been to expose the uniqueness of his thought or to criticize his work. Rather, my primary purpose has been to expose the inner logic of Hartt's theology, the way in which his understanding of the Gospel generates his practice of theology as cultural critique, so that theologians today may appropriate his example.

Since Hartt understands the Gospel of Jesus Christ to be the revelation of the shape of the real world, that is, the revelation of

---

[1]*TMI*, 254.

God and the human situation, theology must attend to culture in order to enable us to see the shape of the real world and live in it. Since the church is that human community commissioned to preach the Gospel in all of its life, theology must attend to the place of the church in the world. Since humans construct worlds that are a mixture of illusion and reality, lies and truth, evil and good, theology must interpret these worlds in the light of the Gospel of Jesus Christ. On these understandings, Hartt rightly practices theology as cultural critique.

Hartt's practice of cultural critique, then, signals his recognition of the situatedness of Christian believing. But that situatedness, in his understanding, is not imposed upon Christianity by the world. Rather, situatedness is given in the very roots of Christianity, in the Gospel itself. And that makes all the difference in the world.

At the beginning of this study, I suggested that Hartt would help us do theology "by the waters of Babylon." What he has taught us is that we are always by the waters of Babylon; and that we are never by the waters of Babylon. More clearly, Hartt has shown us that to think that we are by the waters of Babylon, that is, to think that we are in a foreign land, is to accept the illusions of the world. To believe the Gospel is to see that the shape of the real world is never Babylon, but always the Kingdom of God as established and revealed in Jesus Christ. The Gospel, then, is never the old song; it is never the foreign song; it is the one true song of the divine-human community. Our task is to show the lie that is Babylon by witnessing to and serving the Kingdom of God.

In the preceding chapters, we have looked closely at the substance of Hartt's theology. In summarizing and concluding this study of Hartt's theology, I will briefly examine four aspects of his work which are particularly suggestive for the ongoing work of theology as cultural critique: evangelizing the imagination, transforming history, re-placing metaphysics, and asserting the truth. My purpose here is to identify important elements in Hartt's thought, relate them to other theological proposals in the same areas, and stake out some directions for further development.

• Evangelizing the Imagination •

American culture has long been deeply empirical. For various reasons, this characteristic has given rise, on the one hand, to anti-intellectualism, and, on the other, to the "evasion of philosophy."[2] We want "Just the facts, Ma'am"; we want to be shown. For Americans, "seeing is believing."

Hartt responds to this characteristic with his emphasis on seeing. Rooted in the everlasting actuality of the Kingdom, the Gospel is something to be seen, and the purpose of theology is to enable us to see God.[3] In these assertions, Hartt is guided by the Bible. But Hartt, also knows that what we "see" is shaped by many things. "Everyday," for example, teaches us what we are to "see."[4] In this sense, "believing is seeing." So the language of seeing and of vision must be appropriated critically. What we really need is the imagination to see past the everyday, and the lies and illusions of the world, in order to see the shape of the real world revealed in the Gospel. Our "seeing" must be disciplined by the Gospel; we need an "evangelized imagination."

One review of Hartt's *Theological Method and Imagination* complains that "the title notwithstanding, Hartt has precious little to say about the role of the imagination in theological reflection."[5] While it is true that Hartt does not give explicit, extensive attention to the role of imagination, it is also true that all of Hartt's work is an expression of his understanding of the theological imagination.

For Hartt, theological imagination is not the ability to see something that is not really here, or the ability to project some-

---

[2]Cornel West, *The American Evasion of Philosophy: A Genealogy of Pragmatism* (Madison: University of Wisconsin Press, 1989. What West traces here of the roots of pragmatism may also be said of empiricism. I should add that West's position, like Hartt's, is very critical of empiricism. Indeed, Hartt's theological critique of culture and West's "prophetic pragmatism" bear many similarities.

[3]*TCU*, 134; *TMI*, 18.

[4]*CC*, 21.

[5]George W. Stroup, review of *Theological Method and Imagination* by Julian N. Hartt, in *Theology Today* 34 (October 1978): 337.

thing one wishes were here, or the ability to remake doctrine in order to continue to commend something called Christianity. Rather, theological imagination is the ability to see what really is here; it is the ability to see the Kingdom of God.

Since the Kingdom of God is an everlastingly actual redemption, it must always be in view. But because humanity is captive to the world, to illusions of its own making, humanity's vision of the Kingdom is occluded. Therefore, "the primary goal of that theology called Christian is to amplify the power to see God in all things and thus to participate in the superabundance of his being."[6] In spite of the different vocabulary, this is nothing other than a redescription of Hartt's theological critique of culture. Christian theology amplifies our power to see God in all things by interpreting our culture in the light of the revelation of the Gospel of Jesus Christ, thus exposing the lies and illusions which cloud our vision and enabling our vision of and participation in the Kingdom of God.

Hartt's concern for the actuality of the Kingdom also finds expression in his preference, not always strictly observed, for "vision" rather than "worldview."[7] Vision expresses an intuition of reality and uses metaphor and image to point to that actuality. Worldview is systematic conceptualization of a vision; in other words, worldview is an expansion of a metaphor. However, once developed, worldview may take on a life of its own independent of the vision which gave it birth.

For Hartt, theology is conceptual expansion of the Christian vision of the Kingdom. Theological imagination finds in the Bible the story and images necessary for rightly seeing the Kingdom of God and interpreting our world. Rooted in this vision, and under the discipline of the Holy Spirit in the church, Christian theology appropriates language and concepts from the world which God has created and redeemed in order to show how God's Kingdom is to be made out in the present situation. But the concepts put to

---

[6]*TMI*, 19; cf. 18.
[7]Ibid., 74-77.

work for this purpose are not the rulers of theology or the church; rather, they are to be "evangelized," they are to be ruled by the vision of the Kingdom of God.

This conviction is expressed in Hartt's critique of the errors of systematic theology, his preference for dogmatic theology, and his elevation of practical theology.[8] It is practiced in his interpretation of the Gospel, the church, and the world. Theology, as conceptual development of the vision of the Kingdom of God, should never be allowed to live independently of that vision.[9]

Hartt's understanding of theological imagination is also evident in his description of belief in God as a construing belief. In *The Restless Quest*, Hartt says that belief in God

> is a declaration of intention both to "see" all things as belonging to God and actually so to construe them. Here "construe" is more than a linguistic-intellectual activity. *It means an intention to relate to all things in ways appropriate to their belonging to God.*[10]

Once again Hartt has given a redescription of the convictions expressed in theology as cultural critique. For Hartt, Christian belief in God is rooted in the revelation of the Kingdom in the Gospel of Jesus Christ. Since the Gospel reveals the real shape of the world as God's Kingdom, Christian belief in God commits one to "construing" the whole world as belonging to God. This construal is the work of an imagination formed by the Gospel, that is, it is the work of the "evangelical imagination."

In recent years, theology has increasingly focused on imagination and closely related areas such as vision and aesthetics as fruitful areas for exploration. Hartt's work antedates much of the interest in imagination. Those who early influenced him were Austin Farrer and H. Richard Niebuhr.[11] Hartt takes something from both of these theologians and forges a position different from

---

[8] See chap. 1, s.v., "The Gospel as Foundation."

[9] Cf. *CC*, 134-35, where Hartt argues that "the relation of dependence runs from doctrine to preaching rather than from preaching to doctrine."

[10] *RQ*, 90.

[11] See *TMI*, 16, for allusion to Niebuhr and Farrer.

both. Like Niebuhr, Hartt is concerned with story and images in connection with revelation. Like Farrer, Hartt views the images as mediums of revelation. Hartt's concern for story differentiates him from Farrer; Hartt's view of the images as given by God differentiates him from Niebuhr. As we have seen, Hartt's combination produces fertile consequences for theology as cultural critique.

We may sharpen our understanding of Hartt's use of imagination by juxtaposing him to two contemporary theologians. Gordon Kaufman, who in his first book singles out Niebuhr and Hartt as his teachers, has made much of theological imagination in his recent publications.[12] For Kaufman the theological imagination is constructive, seeking out ways in which theological concepts, particularly the concept of God, can be reconceived for contemporary culture.[13] Kaufman's underlying historicism leads him to assert that

> our theological work need not be constrained in any way by the limitations of earlier interpretations of Christian symbolism. . . . All such earlier articulations of the Christian symbols (including those found in scripture), we can now see, were produced in and through the imaginative activity of men and women of earlier generations, attempting to come to terms with the problems of their lives and their worlds. These are, of course, indispensable in providing insight into the meaning and depth of these symbols, but they are in no way binding on us.[14]

---

[12]For the mention of Hartt, see Gordon D. Kaufman, *Relativism, Knowledge, and Faith* (Chicago: University of Chicago Press, 1960) xii. For his work on imagination see the following works by Kaufman: *An Essay on Theological Method*, revised edition (Missoula: Scholars Press, 1979); *The Theological Imagination: Constructing the Concept of God* (Philadelphia: Westminster Press, 1981); *Theology for a Nuclear Age* (Manchester: Manchester University Press; Philadelphia: Westminster Press, 1985).

[13]Here we will have in view Kaufman's later understanding of the imagination and the work of theology. In his early years, his theological project bears a close resemblance to Hartt's. For a review of Kaufman's development and a thorough critique, see David J. Bryant, *Faith and the Play of Imagination: On the Role of Imagination in Religion*, Studies in American Biblical Hermeneutics 5 (Macon GA: Mercer University Press, 1989) 9-64. Bryant's own account of the theological imagination closely resembles what I will label the "evangelical imagination."

[14]Kaufman, *Theology for a Nuclear Age*, 28.

Thus, Kaufman drops "revelation" as warrant and ground for theological assertions. He now has a "theology of culture" whose purpose is to provide from the contemporary situation symbols and concepts which theology may be permitted to use in its work of imaginative construction.

Hartt agrees with Kaufman that theology is a human work, subject to fallibility and change, but there ends the agreement. Basic to Hartt's differences from Kaufman is Hartt's understanding of the Kingdom as actual, intelligible, and dialectical. Thus, for Hartt the theological imagination is not constructive, it is perceptive.[15] It is that by which humanity grasps, and is grasped by, the Kingdom of God. For Hartt, the images which are a part of the Gospel are binding upon us; theology as conceptualization must always be concerned with its Christian aptness, its fit with the Bible, however problematic that criterion may be.[16] Finally, then, Hartt's theological critique of culture does not grant licensing privileges to contemporary culture for the work of theology. Rather, Hartt's theology is a sustained critique of the lies and illusions of culture in the light of the revelation of Jesus Christ.

Another concept in Hartt's theology that relates to his emphasis on imagination is his description of belief in God as a "construing belief."[17] James Gustafson, a former colleague of Hartt at Yale, has made much of Hartt's notion of "construal." At several crucial points in *Ethics from a Theocentric Perspective*, Gustafson points to Hartt's notion of theology as "a way of construing the world."[18] Gustafson rightly notes that he and Hartt seek to include in

---

[15]Hartt does not enter into any of these debates and thus does not himself use these terms. They are, however, faithful to his work as it has been displayed here.

[16]See David H. Kelsey, *The Uses of Scripture in Recent Theology* (Philadelphia: Fortress Press, 1975).

[17]*RQ*, 90. This is a reprint of an earlier article, Julian N. Hartt, "Encounter and Inference in Our Awareness of God," in Joseph Whelan, ed., *The God Experience: Essays in Hope* (New York: Newman Press, 1971) 30-59.

[18]James M. Gustafson, *Ethics from a Theocentric Perspective. Volume One: Theology and Ethics* (Chicago: University of Chicago Press, 1981) 140. See also 3, 158, 227 (where he describes Hartt's statement as "central to this project"), and 308.

theology affective as well as cognitive elements, that they seek to unify religion and morality, and that for both of them theology is primarily a practical discipline.[19]

But Gustafson's project differs significantly from Hartt's.[20] Much like Kaufman, Gustafson shows little concern to make theology answerable to the Gospel narrative and images or to the church. His concern, rather, is to discern aspects of the Christian tradition which contemporary culture, especially the physical sciences, will permit theology to retrieve and use in its work of reconstruction. For Gustafson, then, theology as "construal" signifies not theology's responsibility to the present actuality of the Kingdom revealed in the Gospel, but rather, theology's responsibility to contemporary culture.

Hartt's work stands clearly over against Gustafson's use of the notion of construal. In Hartt's work, theology as construal stands in dependence upon believing in God. His analysis begins with the claim that belief in God is a construing belief. It announces the believer's intention *"to relate to all things in ways appropriate to their belonging to God."*[21] In applying this assertion to theology, rather than to the believer, Gustafson misuses Hartt's assertion. The misuse is subtle, since Hartt does see theology as a way of construing the world. The misuse lies in Gustafson casting off the primacy of the believer's confession.[22] In the confession of belief in God, the Christian identifies with the community that has been charged with proclaiming the Gospel. The believer is thus under the discipline of the Gospel and the church in ways which Gustafson does

---

[19]Ibid., 158. I am not entirely happy with the terms which Gustafson uses, such as "religion" and "morality," because I do not think they properly represent Hartt's thought. Nevertheless, Gustafson is right to point toward some similarities in his and Hartt's work. So rather than engage in a wrangle over words, I will let them stand. It should be obvious at this point how I think Hartt would respond to some of Gustafson's terms.

[20]See the profound discussion of Gustafson's work between Hartt, Gustafson, and Robert Neville in *Soundings* 73 (Winter 1990): 667-725.

[21]*RQ*, 90. This is a reprint of the essay to which Gustafson refers.

[22]See Gustafson's comment that for him and Hartt, the X from which their theology begins is different. James M. Gustafson, ibid., 696.

not follow. Of course, Gustafson is free to describe theology as a way of construing the world, but his appeal to Hartt should not be taken as a sign of fundamental or extensive agreement in their theology. For Hartt, to describe belief in God as a construing belief binds theology to cultural critique in light of the Gospel. For Gustafson, to describe theology as a way of construing the world binds theology to cultural accommodation in light of the sciences.

By showing how Hartt's understanding of the theological imagination is interdependent with his account of the Kingdom, I am suggesting that Hartt has an "evangelical imagination."[23] His thinking and vision have been so nourished and shaped by the Gospel that he sees more clearly than most the shape of the real world. His strongest argument for and expression of this "evangelical imagination" in theology is his own presentation of the Gospel and critique of the world in the light of the Gospel. There he shows a capacity for vivid metaphor, concrete image, telling rhetoric, which is, finally, not a "method," but a skill, an art. What Hartt's work enjoins upon the theologian who would follow the Gospel, even as does Hartt, is discipline under that Gospel, never forgetting that the Gospel nourishes our imagination and commits us to the church and the world in service to the Kingdom of God.

• Transforming History •

Hartt is profoundly aware that our culture is historicist. That recognition provides one of the pervasive elements in Hartt's theological critique. Yet he is also aware that he must deal with the history of theological approaches to history. According to Hartt's analysis, all of these other approaches are misdirected and in need of a critique.[24] His critique is particularly concerned with the

---

[23]Cf. Donald MacKinnon's essay, "The Evangelical Imagination," in James Mackey, ed., *The Religious Imagination* (Edinburgh: Edinburgh University Press, 1986) 175-85. See also Stanley Hauerwas, *Vision and Virtue: Essays in Christian Ethical Reflection* (Notre Dame IN: Fides, 1974; repr.: Notre Dame IN: University of Notre Dame Press, 1981; and John McIntyre, *Faith, Theology and Imagination* (Edinburgh: Handsel Press, 1987).

[24]*TMI*, chap. 7.

attempts by liberal theology to "salvage" history through reinter-
pretation.[25] What is needed, however, is not an interpretation of
history, but a critique of history in light of the Gospel. This critique
transforms history from creator to creation, from the story that
humans tell to the story that God tells, and in the process it
transforms humanity's being in history.

Hartt's theology contends persistently to accomplish this critique. His re-presentation of the Gospel continually addresses
questions of the historicity of humanity. His ecclesiology lays emphasis on the church's understanding of her own history. And his
critique of the world identifies history as a major element of contemporary culture. Thus, all of Hartt's theology can be seen as a
continual, creative wrestling with varying concepts and issues of
"history."[26]

Hartt never identifies one simple problem of history. Rather,
"history" takes on many different forms, all of which must be subject to a theological critique in the light of the Gospel. Hartt states
this clearly in his analysis of the quarrel over history:

> The Gospel itself is the criterion of plausibility to which every
> philosophical prepossession in the church must yield. Jesus Christ
> contains the definition of historical plausibility; and therefore the
> church is guilty of very great error in elevating a commonsense
> or scientific or metaphysical outlook above that definition.[27]

Thus, in the light of Jesus Christ, history is not the mere passage
of time; it is event-full. History's temporal aspect is not linear or
cyclical; it is periodic. History's consummation is not the mere end
of time; it is the moment when the supreme value, the *telos*, of his-

---

[25]Julian N. Hartt, "Theology as a Hermeneutical Salvaging of History," with
"Commentary" by Arthur C. Danto and "Reflections on Arthur Danto's Commentary" by Hartt, *New Literary History* 17 (Autumn 1986): 183-201.

[26]See also his unpublished Nathaniel W. Taylor Lectures, Julian N. Hartt, "The
One God and the Several Worlds: Faith in God after the End of Salvation
History," Yale Divinity School, 1982.

[27]CC, 281.

tory is revealed.[28] All of these transformations of history draw upon and reveal Hartt's fundamental claim that "history is what God and man have to say to each other. There is sound and fury in it, because man too has a will; but it signifies everything rather than nothing."[29]

These transformations of and fundamental claims about history greatly affect the work of theology. Already we have seen that Hartt sets aside most of the work of historical criticism in his interpretation of the Gospel. Hartt also rejects the claims of "scientific history," of historical evidentialism, of "salvation history," and of historical relativism. In place of these he suggests "story as the art of historical truth," and verisimilitude as the mode of historical truth.[30]

Hartt sees that the significant issue for questions about history is not only "What really happened?" but also "Who did it?"[31] These two questions bring together the issue of factuality and the identity of an agent. Hartt identifies three possible claims which can be made when one is confronted with a historical claim:

1. It was done by X, an unknown party.
2. It could not have happened because the only candidate, the *prima facie* agent, could not have done it. . . .
3. The *prima facie* agent is the real agent; so we must have been mistaken in our first identification of him.[32]"

"Scientific history," he notes, opts for (2) when confronted with the Gospel. Scientific history, then, is really a metaphysical claim, a philosophical argument. At root it is another religion, avoiding such a development only through some pious sleight of hand.[33]

The claims of scientific history have to be met, but not as a position innocent of precommitments. For Hartt, scientific history

---

[28]These sentences are summaries of previous discussion in chaps. 3 and 5.
[29]*CC*, 291.
[30]*TMI*, chaps. 7 and 8.
[31]Ibid., 282.
[32]Ibid., 283.
[33]Ibid., 284.

is something to be brought under the Lordship of Jesus Christ, not something under which his Lordship can be displayed.

Hartt makes short work of the pretensions of historical evidentialism to the establishment of Christ's Lordship. No "strong" case can be made for the full claims of the Gospel on the basis of historical evidence, since the evidence, though fuller than that for most historical claims, already participates in the claims of Christ's Lordship.[34] A strong case can be made for the weaker claims of the Gospel, but these simply assert that Jesus is the one who proclaimed the Kingdom of God. Hartt allows that this may be an intellectually respectable position, but it discards all assertions about Christ's resurrection and his Lordship.[35]

This analysis of "scientific history" and evidentialism makes clear the attractions of historical relativism. Here is a position which, by asserting the relativity of all positions, allows the theologian to continue making claims for the Gospel without having to give (historical) evidence for such claims. However, in a powerful argument that I will not reproduce here, Hartt exposes historical relativism as "an unstable blend of inadvertent metaphysics and incorrigible beliefs relative to historiography."[36] Historical relativism is not the savior of the Gospel which some think it to be.

Against these inferior views of history, Hartt develops a metaphysical theory of history. Hartt begins by distancing himself from Hegel, by disqualifying a priori rejections of metaphysical

---

[34]*TMI*, 166-71.

[35]Ibid., 171.

[36]Ibid., 184. Although he does not mention H. Richard Niebuhr by name, Hartt almost certainly has him in mind. Cf. "Austin Farrer as Philosophical Theologian," 3:

> [Collingwood's] historiographical idealism did much to make historical relativism all but inevitable for many theologians. Witness H. Richard Niebuhr. (Having alluded to him I want to file the opinion that his *Meaning of Revelation* is fundamentally an essay in philosophical theology. His great objective in it is to provide a philosophical foundation and warrant for a confessionalist method in theology.)

We may infer from this quote that Hartt's criticisms of Collingwood are also indirectly addressed to Niebuhr.

theories of history, and by criticizing *heilsgeschichte* theology. Since Hartt is proposing a comprehensive view of history, he must make it clear that Hegel's system is not the only way to go. Against theological objections to a comprehensive view of history, Hartt adduces the cosmological Christ of Colossians. In relation to *heils-geschichte* theology, Hartt acknowledges the primacy of the revelation of Jesus Christ but argues against absolutizing that history to the exclusion of other avenues of historical knowledge. To assert that salvation history is most meaningful does not entail no meaning for other kinds of history.[37]

Hartt's metaphysical theory of history comprises four components which immediately recall his re-presentation of the Gospel in the preaching, person, and work of Jesus Christ. Historical subjecthood, for Hartt, means to have a history, to participate in events over which one has no control. This participation may take shape as one becomes a member of a community whose storied past then becomes one's own story. Historical agency means being the one who gives a community its meaning or the one who intentionally makes some difference to the way things are. Laws of history, on analogy to the law of moral agency, are taken by Hartt to be "a structure of obligation that imparts intelligibility to intentionality."[38] Importance, finally, presupposes a community which assigns value to events and persons.

As a bare sketch, Hartt's "general theory of history" lacks persuasiveness. But when one recalls his discussion of Jesus Christ in these terms, the bare sketch comes alive and exhibits a power and persuasiveness as it takes on the flesh of an actual human life. Thus, Hartt's re-presentation of the Gospel commends his theory of history, rather than his theory of history being a commendation

---

[37]*TMI*, 188-89. Hartt is right, I think, in his critique and correction of salvation history. But given his claim that history is what God and humanity have to say to each other, I am not sure that he is wise to allow for different "kinds" of history.

[38]Ibid., 205.

of the Gospel. History is transformed: history rules no longer; now history is ruled by the Lord who is also its consummation.[39]

For Hartt, theology pursues the truth of history through the art of story.[40] This turn to story is not the last resort of a theology that has recognized the failure of historical evidentialism and accepted the limitations of historical relativism. Rather, Hartt's turn to story is a recognition that story is the way to display historical agency, particularly, in the light of the Gospel, the agency of God and humanity.[41]

On this basis, Hartt criticizes two very different appropriations of story, by Stephen Crites and by Stanley Hauerwas.[42] Although the arguments among Hartt, Crites and Hauerwas are wide ranging and sometimes fall short of clarity, they are instructive, in part because both Crites and Hauerwas acknowledge some indebtedness to Hartt. Two issues seem particularly important in relation to story and the transformation of history.

First, Hartt criticizes Crites for reducing story (and imagination) to the aesthetic. In Hartt's judgment, this move by Crites neglects the historical truth of the Gospel and opens the door to creating a "world" that we imagine, rather than contending with the world created and redeemed by God. Moreover, it seems to obviate the need for a theological critique of the "world" created by lies and illusions. In contrast to this, Hartt sees story as the art of historical truth. That is, story does not sidestep the question of historical truth; rather, it directly engages the questions of historical truth in a way that is faithful to the Gospel of the Kingdom. But theology that is faithful to the Gospel must go

---

[39]Cf. the earlier transformation of human being as history. Only in Jesus Christ do we see that humanity is historical, but not the creation of history. This does not mean that Hartt's theory of history can only be applied to Jesus.

[40]*TMI*, chap. 8.

[41]*TMI*, 238-39.

[42]See the exchange in *JAAR* 52 (Spring 1984): Julian Hartt, "Theological Investments in Story" (117-30), Stephen Crites, "A Respectful Reply to the Assertorical Theologian" (131-39), Stanley Hauerwas, "Why the Truth Demands Truthfulness: An Imperious Engagement with Hartt" (141-47), and Julian Hartt, "Reply to Crites and Hauerwas" (149-56).

beyond telling the story in order to show the import of the story. This is where theology engages other options in a contest for truth, and this is the task that Crites's account seems to neglect.

Secondly, Hartt criticizes Hauerwas for neglecting the metaphysical and ontological dimensions of the Gospel. According to Hartt, story does not argue for or set forth directly a metaphysical system—on this he and Hauerwas agree. However, in Hartt's judgment story does engage "metaphysical convictions," and the Gospel is "full of metaphysical resonances."[43] At some point, as we will see in the following section, theology must give an account of these convictions and resonances. For Hartt it is not sufficient to claim, as Hauerwas does, that "metaphysical issues are more appropriately dealt with indirectly."[44]

Moreover, theology is always contending with other claims to reality. In this contest for the best account of the world, theology must uncover and engage metaphysical and ontological claims, however latent they may be in the competing accounts. This task cannot be accomplished indirectly, through, for example, theological ethics. Rather, since the Gospel contains metaphysical convictions and resonances, we must continually be on guard to repel metaphysical claims that betray, misrepresent, and disable faithful proclamation of the Gospel.

So for Hartt the theological critique of history that discerns its transformation by the Gospel enjoins several tasks. We must argue the historical truth of the Gospel by telling the story of God's redemption of creation through Jesus Christ. We must also argue the historical truth of the Gospel by showing how the Gospel grapples with and redeems the "realities" which we have created and which are imposed upon us. In this we can neglect neither the aesthetic, the ethical, nor the metaphysical.

---

[43]*TMI*, 239, 242.
[44]Stanley Hauerwas, "Why the Truth Demands Truthfulness," 141.

• Re-Placing Metaphysics •

In recent philosophy and theology, the place and practice of metaphysics has become increasingly problematic. In continental philosophy, metaphysics and ontology are seen as discourses of power that sustain and reinforce dominant ideologies and political systems. In America, considerable influence has been exerted by pragmatist critiques of the poverty and triviality of metaphysics. Hartt reflects many of these concerns. For him, founding theology upon a metaphysical system betrays the Gospel and subjects it to an alien power. Moreover, there is a strongly pragmatic cast to his emphasis on practicing the Gospel. Nevertheless, Hartt also recognizes that metaphysical and ontological convictions inevitably shape even those views that seek to deny them. More importantly, metaphysical convictions are required by the Gospel claim that in Jesus Christ, God is revealed. So theology that seeks to be faithful to the Gospel cannot dispense with metaphysics. Rather, theology must assign metaphysics to a new place in its work—metaphysics must be re-placed.

Identifying the "place" of metaphysics in Hartt's theology is a complex matter. One source of the complexity is clearly differentiating metaphysics and philosophy. This is especially important today since so much philosophy is antimetaphysical in mood. It is also important because Hartt does not denigrate the work of philosophy in his theology.[45] The relationship between philosophy and theology may often be framed as an either-or: "Either philosophy is the foundation for and source of a critique of theology or it is of no concern for theology." Hartt pushes a third alternative:

> granted that we cannot extrapolate from the God of the philosophers (ancient, modern, or contemporary) to God in Jesus Christ, are we therefore licensed to say that God in Jesus Christ cannot account for the God of the philosophers? I fear that on this

---

[45] After all, Hartt was Noah Porter Professor of Philosophical Theology at Yale.

matter theologians have confused nonconvertibility with flat irreconcilability.[46]

For Hartt, the dialectic of the Kingdom means that theology must interpret philosophy, as part of culture, in the light of Jesus Christ, in order to discern the good and bad in it. But it is important to note the direction of the critique: theology criticizes philosophy. For this very reason Hartt's theology may appear, at first glance, to be a collection of philosophical positions. But in reality his use of various philosophical insights is disciplined by his understanding of the Gospel, by a kind of purifying critique.[47]

There is a similarity between Hartt's approach to philosophy and his approach to metaphysics. As with philosophy, Hartt rejects an either-or decision: either one accepts metaphysics as the foundation for theology or one rejects metaphysics altogether. Hartt agrees with the rejection of metaphysics as the foundation for theology—when "metaphysics" is used to refer to the variegated tradition of theistic metaphysics which takes as its task the development of categories, concepts, and criteria to which Christian theology must conform. Hartt recognizes that theology has often "taken into its own fabric doctrines from metaphysics, doctrines worked out to meet the logical-speculative requirements of one rational synthesis or another."[48] And he argues that in so doing, theology makes a fundamental error.

But although Hartt rejects "foundation" as the role and place of metaphysics, he does not accept as the only alternative the com-

---

[46]CC, 137. For this reason I have not adverted to Hartt's philosophical work, in particular J. A. C. Fagginger Auer and Julian Hartt, with a foreword by Morris T. Keeton, *Humanism Versus Theism* (Antioch: Antioch Press, 1951; repr. with an introduction by E. D. Klemke: Ames IA: Iowa State University Press, 1981); and *Being Known and Being Revealed*, the 1957 Tully Cleon Knoles Lectures in Philosophy, College of the Pacific Philosophy Institute Publications, vol. 7 (Stockton CA: College of the Pacific Press, 1957).

[47]Here, as elsewhere, Hartt's work brings to mind Paul's ambition to "take every thought captive to obey Christ" (2 Corinthians 10:5 RSV).

[48]CC, 138. Hartt identifies three errors which are noted above, 29n.44.

plete rejection and suppression of metaphysics.[49] Thus, Hartt takes a third alternative by continuing to assert the importance of metaphysical claims but subordinating their conceptual development to the Gospel.

Hartt does not reject metaphysics altogether because he recognizes that "the Gospel story is full of metaphysical resonances."[50] By confessing Jesus as Lord, Christians make metaphysical claims about history and creation. To be sure, the story and the confession are not metaphysical systems, but they do embody metaphysical convictions. To deny those convictions is to diminish Christian believing and reduce the Lordship of Jesus Christ.

Thus, the pressure on theology to find some ready-made scheme springs from the desire to show the relevance of the metaphysical claims of the Gospel. What better way to accomplish that than to show that the Gospel says the same thing as some already accepted conceptual scheme? However, Hartt disciplines the tendency of theology to attach the metaphysical claims of the Gospel story to concepts dependent on some metaphysical system which is independent of the Gospel and then to allow such dependency to blossom into a metaphysical system which becomes the focus of theology. In this situation, the system must be defended and served and witnessed and the Gospel is abandoned.

Against such tendencies, Hartt first provides an account of the Kingdom as actual, intelligible, and dialectical. Since the Kingdom is actual, theology must give some account of how its work corresponds to the Kingdom. Theology is not accountable to any metaphysical system; it is accountable to the Gospel. Since the Kingdom is intelligible, the criterion of relevance presses upon theology, not from any metaphysical scheme, but from the Gospel. But that relevance must be shown through engagement with the metaphysical convictions of the age. Since the Kingdom is God's creation and

---

[49]In this Hartt agrees with Paul Holmer's critique of metaphysics as the foundation of theology, but he parts company when Holmer rejects metaphysics *tout court*. In this Hartt resists any move toward "Wittgensteinian fideism." Cf. Paul L. Holmer, *The Grammar of Faith* (New York: Harper & Row, 1978) esp. 81-110.
[50]*TMI*, 242.

redemption, theology must pursue a critique of the work of meta-physics, discerning the good and the bad, holding fast to the good and putting it to work for the elucidation of the Gospel.

So although Hartt does not reject metaphysics, he does *re-place* it. That is, he moves it from pride of position as the foundation of and authority for theology, to a subordinate position both as an object of critique and as a conceptual articulation of the metaphysi-cal resonances and claims of the Gospel. The primacy which Hartt ascribes to the Gospel as revelation, foundation, and authority, and the preeminence of practical theology discipline the tendency of metaphysics to corrupt the Gospel.[51]

The Gospel story, we have noted, is full of metaphysical claims. And it is this story which is the foundation for the metaphysical work of theology. Again, note the dependence: the conceptual development of theology depends upon the Gospel story which reveals the Kingdom of God. Theology is the display of the coher-ence and the explanatory capabilities of the Gospel, not the first step toward constructing the faith or establishing the bases for its validation. Of course, the elucidation of the sense-making capabil-ity of the Gospel story is precisely what Hartt practices in his theo-logical critique of culture.

• Asserting Truth •

As with metaphysics, theology has increasingly found prob-lems with asserting the truth of the Gospel. We can confess what we believe as Christians, and we can show that Christianity is as rational as any other beliefs, but many problems attend any attempt to assert its truth over against other contenders for truth. Indeed, some radically question the concept of truth as such.

Hartt recognizes the radical reach of these questions, but he is unwilling to give up on truth. In one of his most recent addresses, Hartt recalls the attempt of J. H. Lambert in the 18th century "to pursue systematically issues . . . called *alethiological*" and urges the-

---

[51]See Hartt's various warnings to this effect in *CC*, 165, 187, 192, 341.

ologians to "together plan a faculty seminar in *Alethiology.*"[52] Hartt's own theology is a good place to begin thinking about how to assert the truth of the Gospel in the midst of such radical questioning.

Throughout his work Hartt is concerned with asserting the truth of Christianity in ways that avoid confessionalism and fideism. But as we have seen here, he also seeks to avoid asserting the truth of Christianity on the basis of historical evidentialism and foundationalist metaphysics. In this section, then, I will seek to expose three modes of truth, related to the evangelical imagination, the transformation of history, and the re-placement of metaphysics, which enable Hartt to assert the truth of the Gospel while avoiding confessionalism and fideism.

Hartt's understanding of the evangelical imagination affects all three modes of truth. But the one with which it is most closely, and perhaps unexpectedly, related in Hartt's work is the practice of Christianity.[53] Many aspects of Hartt's theology feed his concern for the practice of Christianity. His emphasis on the three modes of faith, his elevation of practical theology, and his concern for the witness of the church, all reflect and support his emphasis on the practice of the faith.[54]

But his distinctive concern with the practice of Christianity derives from his assertion of the actuality of the Kingdom. Since the Kingdom is an everlasting actuality, there must be signs of it, a real presence of the Kingdom, in the world. And this actuality, this presence, is not available only to eyes of faith which look past "reality" to some posited reality, some future presence. The Kingdom is future, but it is not merely future. It is also actual, here and now, when caring is practiced in the name of Jesus, when

---

[52]"Fallout from Shifts in the Winds of Doctrine," 20, 38.

[53]See *TCU*, 134, where the Kingdom of God is described as "something seen and something to be done."

[54]This emphasis on practice which Hartt carries throughout his work reveals his continuity with the Methodist tradition in which he was raised. Cf. Thomas A. Langford, *Practical Divinity: Theology in the Wesleyan Tradition* (Nashville: Abingdon Press, 1983). Langford summarizes Hartt's contribution on 295n.10.

faith, hope, and love become participation in the Kingdom, and not merely anticipation of it.

In this connection of the practice of Christianity and the actuality of the Kingdom, there is the further relationship to the evangelical imagination. For Hartt the evangelical imagination means seeing the Kingdom of God. Practicing Christianity, then, is making actual the Kingdom of God, so that it may be seen. And making actual the Kingdom of God is verifying, making true, to and through the evangelical imagination, the claims of the Gospel.[55]

Hartt's emphasis on the practice of Christianity is distinguished from many others by his connecting the practice of Christianity to the actuality of the Kingdom and the evangelical imagination. Hartt's is not a vulgar pragmatic test for truth—he does not say that Christianity is true because it works. Rather, he says that because the Gospel asserts the actuality of the Kingdom, the Gospel cannot be true unless the Kingdom is actual—and that means the practice of Christianity. Just as Christ not only preached the Kingdom but also embodied it, those who call him Lord must proclaim the Kingdom, the actual Kingdom, with all their lives. This approach might be called a "traditioned pragmatism," because it is a pragmatism that calls us to practice a way of life rooted in particular convictions about the shape of the real world.

A second mode of truth springs from Hartt's metaphysical theory of history. Here the asserting the truth of the Gospel depends upon story as the art of historical truth and verisimilitude as its criterion. Hartt's metaphysical theory of history depends ultimately on the very particular claim that a new criterion of historical plausibility was established when, in Jesus Christ, God entered into history and now remains in it until the purposes of the Kingdom are fulfilled. The assertion of that claim depends upon the verisimilitude of the story of Jesus Christ.

---

[55]See Hartt, "Theological Investments," the "Reply to Crites and Hauerwas," 156, where he invokes William James notion of "verification as making-true." Hartt adds that James did not say "making-it-up; the will to believe is not to be confused with the will to make believe."

Verisimilitude, says Hartt, is "truthfulness in the aesthetic mode."[56] Thus, to assert the truthfulness of a story is to assert that it re-presents the human situation in a way that we recognize as authentic. A story accomplishes this through its characters, its plot, its texture. One of the tasks of the theologian is to display the verisimilitude of the Gospel—to show how the Gospel story re-presents to us characters and situations in the mundane world which we can recognize as truthful. In doing this, the theologian asserts the aesthetic truthfulness of the Gospel and draws upon the intelligibility of the Kingdom. Such work, Hartt says, must be done at every level of the life of the church. In witnessing to the Gospel, the church must re-present in particular, local ways, the verisimilitude of the Gospel, so that others might find themselves in the story and become participants in the Kingdom.

But here we must confront a crucial issue, for verisimilitude may be a property of fictional stories as well as "reality-intending stories."[57] And the Gospel, in Hartt's understanding, is certainly a reality-intending story—it asserts that something really is the case. Therefore, displaying the verisimilitude of the Gospel is not enough. When the truthfulness of the Gospel is challenged, it is not enough simply to repeat the story, one must take "the metaphysical plunge."[58]

Taking this metaphysical plunge engages the third mode of truth. For Hartt, "taking the metaphysical plunge" does not mean developing a metaphysical system which is not dependent upon Christian convictions, but which establishes their truth. Such a project is doomed to incoherence and failure. Rather, "taking the

---

[56]Hartt, "Theological Investments," 125.

[57]*TMI*, 245. Hartt uses the terms to identify the difference between Faulkner's creation of a verisimilitudinous world in *Absalom! Absalom!* and the claims of the Gospel that, for example, it really is the case that Jesus Christ was raised from the dead.

[58]*RQ*, 13. Here, I think, is where Hartt parts company with Hans Frei. Hartt is very concerned that theology not be content with simply telling and retelling the Gospel story. This concern occurs continually in Hartt's work. Cf. *TMI*, 254; *CC*, 338-44; "Theological Investments in Story"; and a revealing exchange between Hartt, Frei, and others in Dickerman, *Karl Barth and the Future of Theology*, 59-63.

metaphysical plunge" means displaying the explanatory power of the Gospel in relation to the worlds in which we live. The Gospel does not intend a fictional, ideal world which has been "humanely created" by the constructive imaginations of religious thinkers or the church; it intends the real world, a world imposed upon the Gospel.[59]

Here the theologian draws upon the dialectic of the Kingdom in order to make sense of our world in the light of the Gospel. This does not mean finding some rational or psychosocial consensus and then showing how the Gospel conforms to it. Rather, making sense of the world means, for the Christian theologian, interpreting culture, including implicit and explicit metaphysical convictions, in the light of the Gospel in order to show the lies and illusions of the world as well as its truth and reality.

In this comprehensive approach to asserting the truth of the Gospel, Hartt reconfigures the ways in which theology makes a case for that truth. He implicitly accepts various critiques of foundationalism, but he does not abandon the assertive mood. Rather, he gives a coherent and theologically responsible account of the various tasks of theology as it serves the commission of the church everywhere and always "to preach—to show forth, demonstrate, illustrate, and exemplify in every way it can command—the grace of God in Jesus Christ, the same being the mightiest of all powers and the most vital life of all that lives."[60]

---

[59]This is the essence of Hartt's disagreement, on different grounds, with Crites and Hauerwas in "Theological Investments in Story." Crites does not need the Gospel as a "reality-intending" story in order to support the claims created by his rich and engaging imagination. Hauerwas, Hartt suggests, tends toward collapsing claims about what happened to Jesus into claims about the truthfulness of the one's who believe those claims. I think that both Hartt and Hauerwas treat the Gospel as a "reality-intending story." Their disagreement is over the best way to display the truth of that story. Hauerwas argues for "theological ethics" and indirect metaphysics. Hartt wants all of that plus explicit metaphysical argument.

[60]CC, 98.

• Conclusion •

Before I offer a summary critique of Hartt's work, I want to exhibit the profound and properly trinitarian shape to Hartt's theology. Each aspect of Hartt's work which we have examined may be ascribed to one "person" of the Trinity; but each aspect coinheres with other aspects. Our identification of the role of the Gospel as revelation may be ascribed to the Son. The role of the Gospel as foundation properly belongs to the Father. And the Gospel as authority belongs to the work of the Holy Spirit.

Gospel, church, and world may likewise be related to the Trinity: Gospel belonging to Jesus Christ, church belonging to the Spirit, and world belonging to the Father. But as we saw in the course of our study, Gospel, church, and world interpenetrate one another in ways which make it impossible to draw firm boundaries between them. Thus, there is *perichoresis* here, as there is in the Trinity.

The three aspects of the Kingdom which we identified also reflect this trinitarian shape. The actuality of the Kingdom reflects the presence of the Son. The intelligibility of the Kingdom reflects the presence of the Spirit. The dialectic of the Kingdom reflects the presence of the Father. But once again these aspects could be aligned differently. Actuality is property of the Trinity, not just one "person." Intelligibility does not depend on the Spirit alone. And the dialectic is reflected in the Son through whom the Father does all creating, as well as in the Spirit, who restores in us the original plan of creation.

The three modes of truth which we have explored in this chapter can also be shown to have a trinitarian shape.[61] The practice of Christianity relates primarily to the work of the Spirit. The verisimilitude of the Gospel relates to Jesus Christ. And the metaphysical elucidation of the Gospel relates to the work of the

---

[61]I made this suggestion in my original dissertation before I became aware of the work of Bruce D. Marshall, especially *Trinity and Truthfulness* (Cambridge: Cambridge University Press, 1996).

Father. But none of these can stand alone; none is sufficient in itself for asserting the truth of Christianity. Like the Trinity, these modes of truth coinhere. When theology and the church neglect that truth, the faith itself is attenuated and Gospel, church, and world suffer.

In my construal of Hartt's theology I have attempted to display the strengths of his work and I have indicated along the way some of the weaknesses I see in it. Here I will bring into focus those strengths and weaknesses.

Hartt's uses of the Gospel as revelation, foundation and authority are, in my judgment, exactly right. His development of these aspects deftly shifts emphases, reorders priorities, and assimilates insights from other positions in ways that open up new possibilities, new vistas for the work of theology and the mission of the church. These possibilities and vistas are immediately evident in Hartt's interpretation of the Gospel, church, and world. Again, I think these three are precisely the aspects necessary to Christian theology.

In Hartt's interpretation of the Gospel, his use of "participation" language in his christology is a bold, illuminating effort to elucidate a biblical christology in language other than that of the metaphysics of substance. This is one aspect of his work which deserves more careful, critical attention than I have been able to give it in this broad treatment of his work. In my judgment, his Christology points in the direction that theology which seeks to be faithful to the Gospel must always be moving, taking captive to Christ the thought of the world.

Another strength of Hartt's theology is his recognition that elucidation of the Gospel necessarily involves interpretation of the world. This recognition, of course, leads him to theology as cultural critique. In this way, all of Hartt's theology is elucidation of the Gospel. In its narrower focus, the central section of *A Christian Critique of American Culture*, which I presented in chapter 3, is Hartt's elucidation of the Gospel.

In his re-presentation of the Gospel, Hartt shows how the Gospel grapples with the "ontological fundamentals" of human existence. Hartt's lack of clarity here is one which raises several questions about his theology. First, he does not immediately guard himself from the appearance that these ontological fundamentals are the criteria by which the Gospel is to be judged. Only when he later begins to interpret and transform those fundamentals by the light of the Gospel is it clear that they are not criteria, but material for the proclamation of the Gospel. Secondly, Hartt abruptly introduces the five ontological fundamentals (death, anxiety, creativity, love, and guilt). From where do they come? Did Hartt dream them up? Are they the product of phenomenological analysis? Does he take them from the work of another philosopher? Does scripture delineate them? Are they entailed by Christian understanding of creation and redemption? Why these five elements? Are they also the essentials of non-Western cultures? Does the use of different characterizations to elucidate the identity of Christ the preacher indicate a certain flexibility?[62]

Although Hartt leaves himself open to these questions, I think he is right to insist upon an ontological perspective as indispensable in the elucidation of the Gospel. Even with an emphasis on narrative and human being as history, theology must give some account of human relationship to various structures, in various contexts. These structures and contexts do not have to be universal categories, abstractions, or foundationalist claims; nor need they always travel under the name of ontology. They can be local, particular, *ad hoc*; they can travel under the name of ethics. Although Hartt does not use them in these ways, and in his exchange with Hauerwas resists this move, his own interpretation of the human essence as projective, as historical, pushes in this direction and provides some markers along the way.

Finally, the three aspects of the Kingdom which run through Hartt's theology supply much of its strength and creativity. As they coinhere, they guard his theology from dangers threatened by any one aspect taken alone. His understanding of the actuality of the Kingdom guards intelligibility from becoming a shallow quest for relevance and guards the dialectic from becoming a recipe for

---

[62]*CC*, 188-98.

nostalgia and traditionalism. His understanding of the intelligibility of the Kingdom prevents the actuality of the Kingdom from becoming the private possession of an enlightened elite and prevents the dialectic from becoming intellectual gamesmanship. The dialectic of the Kingdom ensures that the actuality and intelligibility of the Kingdom does not become a rationale either for uncritical acceptance and approval of the world or for uncritical rejection and condemnation of the world.

Hartt's understanding of the church evinces three strengths: his careful delineation of the relationship between the Kingdom and the church; his rejection of a Constantinian view of the relationship between church and society; and his interpretations of the life of the church in "Christian civilization." Hartt's ecclesiology is weak in two areas. First, he does not attend to the concrete aspects of the life of a community which are necessary for fulfilling the mission of the church.[63] This is a serious omission since Hartt places such heavy demands upon the church as the community where the vision of the Kingdom comes to life so that the human situation is rightly discerned. However, this omission does not call his ecclesiology into question; it merely points to more work which needs to be done. Secondly, in a related matter, Hartt does not attend as closely as he should to the material conditions of the life of the church in Western culture. One does not have to be a Marxist in order to recognize and decry the penetration of the church by affluence and consumerism. In the midst of this, what does God demand—materially—from the church in order for her to discern the Kingdom?

The great strength of Hartt's critique of "world" is his systematic attention to the situation in which the church lives and the Gospel is proclaimed and the persistently *ad hoc* approach to whatever shape and color the world comes in. Hartt's various critiques embody these strengths and discern the illusions and realities of the human situation. One weakness in his critique is again the absence of sustained attention to the material conditions of life in

---

[63]Though see, in this regard, the brief, suggestive discussion in *TCU*, 138-61.

Western society. His comparison of covenant and contract, community and corporation, though suggestive, is primarily descriptive. Given Hartt's rhetorical powers, we must regret the absence of a sustained critique of the material conditions of our society.[64]

The other weakness in Hartt's critique of the world is his failure to attend to "scientific" culture as thoroughly as he does "artistic" culture. Of course, no one thinker can do it all, and Hartt has done as much as anyone in our age, but the failure to mount a significant critique of scientific creativity leaves open the possibility that Hartt's theology can manage the humanities but not the sciences. I do not think that this is the case, but that remains to be shown.[65]

The four aspects of Hartt's methodology which I analyzed earlier in this chapter are four pressure points in contemporary debate. Hartt's emphasis on the imagination is rightly grounded in the actuality of the Kingdom. His transformation of history, together with his elucidation of the verisimilitude of the Gospel, provide a powerful alternative to other construals of the relationship between theology and history. His replacement of metaphysics rightly seeks to retain one aspect of the claims of the Gospel without eviscerating those claims in the attempt to assert them. And his threefold assertion of the truth reflects the various aspects of his theology which I have already affirmed.

However, each of these points can be strengthened. In Hartt's emphasis on imagination I miss an explication of revelation as imaginal. On this topic, Hartt alludes to both Austin Farrer and H. Richard Niebuhr. His rejection of confessionalism and historicism

---

[64]After twice registering the omission of attention to material conditions of the church and of Western culture, I must express the suspicion that Hartt's commitment to his five ontological fundamentals restrict his freedom of analysis here. His critique of modernity does recognize the importance of material conditions, but he does not carry description through to criticism.

[65]A comparison of Gustafson and Hartt is very suggestive here. For all the similarities in their purposes, they produce very different theologies. Is there something to be learned from Gustafson's focusing on the sciences and Hartt's focusing on the humanities? Of course this is not the only, or even the crucial, difference between them.

distances him from Niebuhr. On other points he approaches Farrer, but his interpretation of the Gospel is very different from that found in Farrer's commentaries. How, then, are we to understand the biblical images as revelation? Apart from his use of the Kingdom of God, Hartt gives us little guidance. Are there master images in the Bible? Is the Kingdom a (the) master image? If there is a master image, how are other images related to it?[66]

Hartt's transformation of history cries out for a more thorough critique of the other options.[67] Such critique could build on the bases which Hartt has laid down—what we need are not new bases, but more thorough criticism. At the same time, the constructive side of Hartt's transformation should not be neglected. But here what is needed is not more critics, but more artists, not more attention to methodology, but more elucidations of the verisimilitude of the Gospel story.

Hartt's re-placement of metaphysics raises, for me, some of the strongest questions. He is persuasive in his arguments for the rejection of metaphysics as the foundation or authority for theology. And I agree with his desire to assert and defend Christian convictions about divine agency in the Gospel story. But I suspect that embedded in the very nature and tradition of metaphysics is the conviction that metaphysics bows to no one, that metaphysics is born to rule.[68] Hartt may then kick metaphysics out the front door,

---

[66]Here I must note Ray L. Hart's *Unfinished Man and the Imagination: Toward an Ontology and a Rhetoric of Revelation* (New York: Seabury Press, 1979), which is a major revision of a dissertation on Austin Farrer supervised by Julian Hartt. I have not given it more attention because a fair comparison of the two thinkers would require that I give extensive space to an interpretation of Hart's recondite work. Such attention might well prove rewarding, but it would lead me away from my purposes.

[67]See here Hartt's Nathaniel Taylor Lectures.

[68]I am thinking here of Michael J. Buckley's magisterial volume, *At the Origins of Modern Atheism* (New Haven CT: Yale University Press, 1987). Buckley's work tells the story of the subversion of theology by philosophy. Like Hartt, Buckley wants to locate metaphysics within the context of christology and pneumatology (361). But what impresses me about the story is how willingly theology submitted to its own subversion. I am not at all convinced that theology is armed against a reoccurrence.

but he lets it in the back door by continuing to engage in explicit metaphysical argument. Hartt may be strong enough to keep metaphysics in a subordinate role, but will the next theologian?

What would have been particularly fruitful here is an explication by Hartt of the interrelationship of images, story, and metaphysics. These three are seldom found in combination in a theologian, yet the fertility and power of Hartt's theology suggests that there may be considerable profit in an investigation of their interrelationships. Again, Hartt has laid out a path in a direction which should be explored further.

So our study of Hartt's theology raises many questions. These questions are not signs of fundamental weakness in Hartt's work. Rather, they are signs of his creativity and of the unfinished character of theology as cultural critique. In the logic of his position, in the central elements of his theology, and in his interpretation of Gospel, church, and world, Hartt has shows us creative and fertile directions for theology. The strengths and weaknesses which I have discerned in Hartt's theology are not really the conclusion of our study, but rather its commencement. Resources for pursuing the questions I have raised and for strengthening the weaknesses I have suggested lie within Hartt's own work.

Julian Hartt's practice of theology as cultural critique is a never-ending quest to interpret the world in the light of the Gospel of Jesus Christ in order that humanity might participate in the Kingdom of God. Julian Hartt pursues that theological quest with passion, originality, and vision. May we learn from him how better to do theology and in that doing witness and serve the Kingdom which is the joy of all desiring.

Selected Bibliography

• Works by Julian Hartt •

• A. Books •

Being Known and Being Revealed. Tulley Cleon Knoles Lectures in Philosophy. Volume 7. Stockton CA: College of the Pacific Philosophy Institute Publications, 1957.

A Christian Critique of American Culture: An Essay in Practical Theology. New York: Harper & Row, 1967.

The Lost Image of Man. Baton Rouge: Louisiana State University Press, 1963.

The Restless Quest. Philadelphia: United Church Press, 1975.

Theological Method and Imagination. New York: Seabury Press, A Crossroad Book, 1977.

Theology and the Church in the University. Philadelphia: Westminster Press, 1969.

Toward a Theology of Evangelism. New York: Abingdon Press, 1955.

With Ray L. Hart and Robert P. Scharlemann. *The Critique of Modernity: Theological Reflections on Contemporary Culture*. Charlottesville: University Press of Virginia, 1986.

With J. A. C. Fagginger Auer. *Humanism versus Theism*. Foreword by Morris T. Keeton. Antioch OH: Antioch Press, 1951; repr.: with an introduction by E. D. Klemke: Ames: Iowa State University Press, 1981.

• B. Articles •

"Albert Camus: An Appreciation." *Christianity and Crisis* 20 (8 February 1960): 7-8.

"Austin Farrer as Philosophical Theologian: A Retrospective and Appreciation." In *For God and Clarity: New Essays in Honor of Austin Farrer*, 1-22. Edited by Jeffrey C. Eaton and Ann Loades. Allison Park PA: Pickwick Publications, 1983.

"Christian Faith and Our World." *Social Action* 18 (October 1951): 3-39.

"Christian Freedom Reconsidered: The Case of Kierkegaard." *Harvard Theological Review* 60 (April 1967): 133-44.

"A Commentary on Fox's Diagnosis of the Human Condition," [Journal]: 59-77.

"Concerning God and Man and His Well-Being: A Commentary, Inspired by Spinoza, on Gustafson's *Ethics from a Theocentric Perspective,*" *Soundings* 73 (Winter 1990): 667-87.

"Creation and Providence." In *Christian Theology: An Introduction to Its Traditions and Tasks,* edited by Robert H. King and Peter C. Hodgson, 115-40. Philadelphia: Fortress Press, 1982.

"Dialectic, Analysis, and Empirical Generalization in Theology." *Crozer Quarterly* 29 (January 1952): 1-17.

"Encounter and Inference in Our Awareness of God." In *The God Experience: Essays in Hope,* edited by Joseph P. Whelan, 30-59. New York: Newman Press, 1971. Reprinted in *The Restless Quest,* 73-95.

"The Ethics of Dissent." *Theology Today* 23 (January 1967): 496-504. Reprinted in *The Restless Quest,* 135-42.

"God, Transcendence and Freedom in the Philosophy of Jaspers." *Review of Metaphysics* 4 (December 1950): 247-58.

"Hubert Humphrey and the Pieties of the Prairie (Memories of Doland, S.D.)." *Dialog* (Minnesota) 23 (Summer 1984): 174-82.

"Human Freedom and Divine Transcendence." *Journal of Religion* 31 (January 1951): 38-51.

"Metaphysics, History, and Civilization: Collingwood's Account of Their Interrelationships." *Journal of Religion* 33 (July 1953): 198-211.

"Modern Images of Man." *The Central Conference of American Rabbis Journal* (June 1969), 2-17. Reprinted in *The Restless Quest,* 117-34.

"Moral Unintelligibility: A Commentary on the Asbury-Hauerwas Debate," *Soundings* 76 (Winter 1993): 591-602.

"Objectivity vs. Faithfulness: A Running Contest in Teaching Religion." *Perspectives in Religious Studies* 5 (Summer 1978): 76-84.

"An Overview." In *Karl Barth and the Future of Theology,* 40-44. A Memorial Colloquium Held at the Yale Divinity School, January 28, 1969. Edited by David L. Dickerman. New Haven CT: Yale Divinity School Association, 1969.

"The Philosopher, the Prophet, and the Church (Some Reflections on Their Roles as Critics of Culture)." *Journal of Religion* 35 (July 1955): 147-59. Reprinted in *The Restless Quest,* 33-49.

"The Pursuit of Practical Theology." *Drew Gateway* 39 (Autumn 1968): 16-28.

"Secularity and the Transcendence of God." In *Secularization and the Protestant Prospect*, 151-73. Edited with an introduction by James F. Childress and David Harned. Philadelphia: Westminster Press, 1970. Reprinted in *The Restless Quest*, 97-113.

"The Significance of Despair in Contemporary Theology." *Theology Today* 13 (April 1956): 45-62.

"The Situation of the Believer." In *Faith and Ethics: The Theology of H. Richard Niebuhr*, edited by Paul Ramsey, 225-44. New York: Harper & Brothers, 1957.

"Some Metaphysical Gleanings from Prayer." *Journal of Religion* 31 (October 1951): 254-63.

"Theological Investments in Story: Some Comments on Recent Developments and Some Proposals." Replies by Stephen Crites and Stanley Hauerwas. Reply by Julian Hartt. *Journal of the American Academy of Religion* 52 (March 1984): 117-56.

"The Theological Situation After Fifty Years." *Yale Review* 51 (Autumn 1961): 75-101.

"Theology as a Hermeneutical Salvaging of History." With commentary by Arthur C. Danto and reflections on Arthur Danto's commentary by the author. *New Literary History* 17 (Autumn 1986): 183-201.

"Theology of Culture." *Review of Metaphysics* 6 (March 1953): 501-10.

"Thoughts Prompted by Neville's Commentary," *Soundings* 73 (Winter 1990): 719-25.

"William Faulkner: An Appreciation." *Christianity and Crisis* 22 (August 6, 1962): 137-38.

• C. Review Articles •

Faith and Reason: Essays in the Philosophy of Religion by R. G. Collingwood. *Journal of Religion* 49 (July 1969): 280-94.

The Logic of Perfection by Charles Hartshorne. *Review of Metaphysics* 16 (June 1963): 749-69.

"The Loss of Normativeness." Review of *The Age of Malaise* by Dacia Maraine; *Textures of Life* by Hortense Calisher; *Morte D'Urban*, by J. F. Powers; *Elizabeth Appleton* by John O'Hara; and *The Unicorn* by Iris Murdoch. *The Christian Scholar* 47 (Summer 1964): 176-83.

"On the Possibility of an Existentialist Philosophy." Review of *The Ethics of Ambiguity* by Simone De Beauvoir; *The Philosophy of Existence* by Gabriel Marcel; *Encounter with Nothingness* by Helmut Kuhn; *Existentialism* by Ralph Harper; *The Emotions* by Jean-Paul Sartre; *Existentialisme et Pensee Chretienne* by Roger Troisfontaines; and *A Short History of Existentialism* by Jean Wahl. *Review of Metaphysics* 3 (September 1949): 95-106.

"The Realities of the Human Situation." Review of *Personal Knowledge: Towards a Post-Critical Philosophy* by Michael Polanyi. *The Christian Scholar* 43 (Fall 1960): 231-36.

• D. Unpublished Material •

"Fall-out from Shifts in the Winds of Doctrine." Lecture, 1988. (Photocopied.)

"The One God and the Several Worlds: Faith in God after the End of Salvation History." Nathaniel W. Taylor Lectures, Yale Divinity School, 1982. (Taped.)

"The Ontological Argument for the Existence of God: A Historicocritical Exposition of Some of Its Metaphysical and Epistemological Issues." Ph.D. dissertation, Yale University, 1940.

• Other Sources •

Anderson, Ray S. *Historical Transcendence and the Reality of God*. Grand Rapids MI: Eerdmans, 1975.

Becker, Ernst. *The Denial of Death*. New York: Free Press, 1973.

Berkhof, Hendrikus. *Christ and the Powers*. Scottdale PA: Herald Press, 1962.

Bonhoeffer, Dietrich. *Letters and Papers from Prison*. Enlarged edition. Translated by Eberhard Bethge. London: SCM Press, 1971.

Brown, Colin. *Jesus in European Protestant Thought 1778–1860*. Durham NC: Labyrinth Press, 1987.

Bryant, David J. *Faith and the Play of Imagination. On the Role of Imagination in Religion*. Studies in American Biblical Hermeneutics 5. Macon GA: Mercer University Press, 1989.

Buckley, Michael J. *At the Origins of Modern Atheism*. New Haven CT: Yale University Press, 1987.

Burrell, David. *Aquinas: God and Action*. Notre Dame IN: University of Notre Dame Press, 1979.

Calvin, Jean. *Institutes of the Christian Religion*. Two volumes. Edited by John T McNeill. Translated by Ford Lewis Battles. Philadephia: Westminster Press, 1960.

Campbell, Dennis M. *Authority and the Renewal of American Theology*. Philadelphia: United Church Press, 1976.

Collingwood, R. G. *Essay on Metaphysics*. Oxford: Oxford University Press, 1940.

Crites, Stephen. "The Narrative Quality of Experience." *Journal of the American Academy of Religion* 39 (September 1971): 291-311.

_____. "Unfinished Figure: On Theology and the Imagination." In *Unfinished . . . : Essays in Honor of Ray Hart*, edited by Mark C. Taylor, 155-84. JAAR Thematic Studies 48. Chico CA: Scholars Press.

Cunningham, David S. *Faithful Persuasion: In Aid of a Rhetoric of Christian Theology*. Notre Dame IN: University of Notre Dame Press, 1992.

Dickerman, David L., ed. *Karl Barth and the Future of Theology*. A memorial colloquium held at Yale Divinity School, 28 January 1969. New Haven CT: Yale Divinity School Association, 1969.

Dulles, Avery. *Models of the Church*. Expanded edition. Garden City NY: Image Books (Doubleday), 1987.

Farrer, Austin. *Finite and Infinite: A Philosophical Essay*. Second edition. Westminster: Dacre Press; New York: Seabury Press, A Crossroad Book, 1979.

_____. *The Glass of Vision*. Westminster: Dacre Press, 1948.

Frei, Hans W. *The Eclipse of Biblical Narrative: A Study in Eighteenth and Nineteenth Century Hermeneutics*. New Haven CT: Yale University Press, 1974.

_____. *The Identity of Jesus Christ: The Hermeneutical Bases of Dogmatic Theology*. Philadelphia: Fortress Press, 1975.

_____. "The Theology of H. Richard Niebuhr." In *Faith and Ethics: The Theology of H. Richard Niebuhr*, edited by Paul Ramsey, 65-116. New York: Harper & Brothers, 1957.

Goldberg, Michael. "God, Action, and Narrative: *Which* Narrative? *Which* Action? *Which* God?" *Journal of Religion* 68 (January 1988): 39-56.

Gustafson, James M. *Can Ethics Be Christian?* Chicago: University of Chicago Press, 1975.

_____. *Ethics from a Theocentric Perspective*. Volume 1. *Theology and Ethics*. Chicago: University of Chicago Press, 1981.

_____. "Response to Hartt." *Soundings* 73 (Winter 1990): 689-700.

Hart, Ray L. *Unfinished Man and the Imagination: Toward an Ontology and a Rhetoric of Revelation*. New York: Seabury Press, 1979.

Harvey, Van A. *The Historian and the Believer: The Morality of Knowledge and Christian Belief*. New York: Macmillan, 1966; repr.: Philadelphia: Westminster Press, 1981.

Hauerwas, Stanley. *Against the Nations: War and Survival in a Liberal Society*. Minneapolis: Winston Press, 1985.

_____. "The Church as God's New Language." In *Scriptural Authority and Narrative Interpretation*, edited by Garrett Green, 179-98. Philadelphia: Fortress Press, 1987.

_____. *A Community of Character: Toward a Constructive Christian Social Ethic*. Notre Dame IN: University of Notre Dame Press, 1981.

_____. *The Peaceable Kingdom: A Primer in Christian Ethics*. Notre Dame IN: University of Notre Dame Press, 1983.

_____. *Vision and Virtue: Essays in Christian Ethical Reflection*. Notre Dame IN: Fides, 1974; repr.: Notre Dame IN: University of Notre Dame Press, 1981.

Holmer, Paul L. *The Grammar of Faith*. New York: Harper & Row, 1978.

Jones, L. Gregory. *Transformed Judgment: Toward a Trinitarian Account of the Moral Life*. Notre Dame IN: University of Notre Dame Press, 1990.

Kähler, Martin. *The So-Called Historical Jesus and the Historic Biblical Christ*. Foreword by Paul Tillich. Translated, edited, and with an introduction by Carl E. Braaten. Seminar editions. Philadelphia: Fortress Press, 1964.

Kaufman, Gordon D. *An Essay on Theological Method*. Revised edition. Missoula MT: Scholars Press, 1979.

_____. *Relativism, Knowledge, and Faith*. Chicago: University of Chicago Press, 1960.

_____. *Theology for a Nuclear Age*. Manchester: Manchester University Press; Philadelphia: Westminster Press, 1985.

_____. *The Theological Imagination: Constructing the Concept of God*. Philadelphia: Westminster Press, 1981.

Kelsey, David H. "Christian Sense Making: Hartt's *Theological Method and Imagination*. *Journal of Religion* 58 (October 1978): 428-35.

_____. *The Fabric of Paul Tillich's Theology*. Yale Publications in Religion 13. New Haven CT: Yale University Press, 1967.

_____. *The Uses of Scripture in Recent Theology*. Philadelphia: Fortress Press, 1975.

Langford, Thomas A. *Practical Divinity: Theology in the Wesleyan Tradition*. Nashville: Abingdon Press, 1983.

Lash, Nicholas. *Voices of Authority*. Shepherdstown WV: Patmos Press, 1976.

_____. *Easter in Ordinary: Reflections on Human Experience and the Knowledge of God*. Charlottesville: University Press of Virginia, 1988.

Lessing, Gotthold. *Lessing's Theological Writings*. Edited with an introduction by Henry Chadwick. Stanford CA: Stanford University Press, 1972.

Lewis, C. S. "Meditation in a Toolshed." In *God in the Dock,* edited with an introduction by Walter Hooper, 212-15. Grand Rapids MI: Eerdmans, 1974.

Lindbeck, George. *The Nature of Doctrine: Religion and Theology in a Postliberal Age.* Philadelphia: Westminster Press, 1984.

McClendon, James William, Jr. *Ethics: Systematic Theology.* Volume 1. Nashville: Abingdon Press, 1986.

MacIntyre, Alasdair. *After Virtue.* Second edition. Notre Dame IN: University of Notre Dame Press, 1984.

McIntyre, John. *Faith, Theology and Imagination.* Edinburgh: Handsel Press, 1987.

MacKinnon, Donald. "The Evangelical Imagination." In *The Religious Imagination,* edited by James P. Mackey. Edinburgh: Edinburgh University Press, 1986.

Marshall, Bruce D. *Christology in Conflict: The Identity of a Saviour in Rahner and Barth.* Oxford: Basil Blackwell, 1987.

_____. *Trinity and Truthfulness.* Cambridge: Cambridge University Press, 1996.

Michalson, Gordon E., Jr. *Lessing's "Ugly" Ditch: A Study of Theology and History.* University Park: Pennsylvania State University Press, 1985.

Mitchell, Basil. *The Justification of Religious Belief.* New York: Seabury Press, 1973.

Niebuhr, H. Richard, in collaboration with Daniel Day Williams and James M. Gustafson. *The Purpose of the Church and Its Ministry.* New York: Harper & Brothers, 1956.

_____. *Christ and Culture.* New York: Harper & Row, 1951.

_____. *The Meaning of Revelation.* New York: MacMillan, 1941.

Pannenberg, Wolfhart. *Theology and the Kingdom of God.* Philadelphia: Westminster Press, 1969.

_____. *Jesus: God and Man.* Second edition. Translated by Lewis L. Wilkins and Duane A. Priebe. Philadelphia: Westminster Press, 1977.

Rahner, Karl. *Foundations of Christian Faith: An Introduction to the Idea of Christianity.* Translated by William V. Dych. New York: Crossroad, 1987.

Schell, Jonathan. *The Fate of the Earth.* New York: Alfred A. Knopf, 1982.

Scriven, Michael. *The Transformation of Culture: Christian Social Ethics After H. Richard Niebuhr.* Foreword by James Wm. McClendon, Jr. Scottdale PA: Herald Press, 1987.

Smith, D. Moody, Jr. "The Historical Jesus in Paul Tillich's Christology." *Journal of Religion* 46 (January 1966): 131-47.

Stout, Jeffrey. *The Flight from Authority: Religion, Morality, and the Quest for Autonomy.* Notre Dame IN: University of Notre Dame Press, 1981.

Stroup, George W. Review of *Theological Method and Imagination* by Julian N. Hartt. *Theology Today* 34 (October 1978): 337-38.

Surin, Kenneth. *Turnings of Darkness and Light: Essays in Philosophical and Systematic Theology.* Cambridge: Cambridge University Press, 1989.

Thiemann, Ronald F. *Revelation and Theology.* Notre Dame IN: University of Notre Dame Press, 1985.

Troeltsch, Ernst. *Ernst Troeltsch: Writings on Theology and Religion.* Edited with additional essays by Robert Morgan and Michael Pye. Atlanta: John Knox Press, 1977.

West, Cornel. *The American Evasion of Philosophy: A Genealogy of Pragmatism.* Madison: University of Wisconsin Press, 1989.

_____. *Keeping Faith: Philosophy and Race in America.* New York: Routledge, 1993.

Wilson, Jonathan R. "From Theology of Culture to Theological Ethics: The Hartt-Hauerwas Connection," *Journal of Religious Ethics* 23 (Spring 1995): 149-64.

_____. "The Gospel as Revelation in Julian N. Hartt," *Journal of Religion* 72 (October 1992): 549-59.

_____. *Gospel Virtues: Practicing Faith, Hope, and Love in Uncertain Times.* Downers Grove IL: InterVarsity Press, 1997.

_____. *Living Faithfully in a Fragmented World: Four Lessons for the Church from MacIntyre's "After Virtue."* Valley Forge PA: Trinity Press International, 1996.

_____. "Revising Macintosh by Hartt: Shaping Empirical Theology," *Perspectives in Religious Studies* (Spring 1993): 43-55.

Wilson, William McFetridge. "A Different Method; A Different Case: The Theological Program of Julian Hartt and Austin Farrer." *The Thomist* 53 (October 1989): 599-633.

Wood, Charles M. *The Formation of Christian Understanding: An Essay in Theological Hermeneutics.* Philadelphia: Westminster Press, 1981.

Yoder, John Howard, Diane M. Yeager, and Glen H. Stassen. *Authentic Transformation: A New Vision of Christ and Culture.* Nashville: Abingdon Press, 1996.

_____. *The Politics of Jesus: Vicit Agnus Noster.* Grand Rapids MI: Eerdmans, 1972.

_____. *The Priestly Kingdom: Social Ethics as Gospel.* Notre Dame IN: University of Notre Dame Press, 1984.

Theology as Cultural Critique.
The Achievement of Julian Hartt.
  by Jonathan R. Wilson.
Studies in American Biblical Hermeneutics 12 (StABH 12).

Mercer University Press, Macon, Georgia 31210-3960
Isbn 0-86554-522-7. Catalog and warehouse pick number: MUP/P148.
Text and cover designs, composition, and layout by Edd Rowell.
Camera-ready pages composed on a Gateway 2000
  via WordPerfect 5.1/5.2 and printed on a LaserMaster 1000.
Text font: (Adobe) Palatino 11/13 and 10/12.
Display font: (Adobe) Palatino 24-, 12-, and 11-point bf.
Printed and bound by McNaughton & Gunn Inc., Saline MI 48176.
  Printed via offset lithography on 50# Writers Natural (500ppi).
  Perfectbound in 10-pt. c1s stock,
    printed one color (PMS 497), and lay-flat film laminated.
[November 1996]